T0213711

In-Memory Data Management Research

Series editor

Prof. Dr. Dr. h.c. Hasso Plattner
Hasso Plattner Institute
Potsdam, Germany

More information about this series at http://www.springer.com/series/11642

Christian Tinnefeld

Building a Columnar Database on RAMCloud

Database Design for the Low-Latency
Enabled Data Center

 Springer

Christian Tinnefeld
Hasso Plattner Institute
University of Potsdam
Potsdam
Germany

ISSN 2196-8055   ISSN 2196-8063   (electronic)
In-Memory Data Management Research
ISBN 978-3-319-37389-8   ISBN 978-3-319-20711-7   (eBook)
DOI 10.1007/978-3-319-20711-7

Springer Cham Heidelberg New York Dordrecht London
© Springer International Publishing Switzerland 2016
Softcover reprint of the hardcover 1st edition 2016

Printed on acid-free paper

Springer International Publishing AG Switzerland is part of Springer Science+Business Media
(www.springer.com)

*I thank my parents Gerd and Margret
for their love and support*

Preface

In the field of disk-based parallel database management systems exists a great variety of solutions based on a shared-storage or a shared-nothing architecture. In contrast, main memory-based parallel database management systems are dominated solely by the shared-nothing approach as it preserves the in-memory performance advantage by processing data locally on each server. We argue that this unilateral development is going to cease due to the combination of the following three trends: (a) Nowadays, network technology features remote direct memory access (RDMA) and narrows the performance gap between accessing main memory inside a server and of a remote server to and even below a single order of magnitude. (b) Modern storage systems scale gracefully, are elastic, and provide high-availability. (c) A modern storage system such as Stanford's RAMCloud even keeps all data resident in main memory. Exploiting these characteristics in the context of a main-memory parallel database management system is desirable. The advent of RDMA-enabled network technology makes the creation of a parallel main memory DBMS based on a shared-storage approach feasible.

This work describes building a columnar database on shared main memory-based storage. It discusses the resulting architecture (Part I), the implications on query processing (Part II), and presents an evaluation of the resulting solution in terms of performance, high-availability, and elasticity (Part III).

We use Stanford's RAMCloud as shared-storage, and the self-designed and developed in-memory AnalyticsDB as relational query processor on top. AnalyticsDB encapsulates data access and operator execution via an interface which allows seamless switching between local and remote main memory, while RAMCloud provides not only storage capacity, but also processing power. Combining both aspects allows pushing-down the execution of database operators into the storage system. We describe how the columnar data processed by AnalyticsDB is mapped to RAMCloud's key-value data model and how the advantages of columnar data storage can be preserved.

The combination of fast network technology and the possibility to execute database operators in the storage system opens the discussion for site selection. We construct a system model that allows the estimation of operator execution costs in terms of network transfer, data processed in memory, and wall time. This can be used for database operators that work on one relation at a time—such as a scan or materialize operation—to discuss the site selection problem (data pull vs. operator push). Since a database query translates to the execution of several database operators, it is possible that the optimal site selection varies per operator. For the execution of a database operator that works on two (or more) relations at a time, such as a join, the system model is enriched by additional factors such as the chosen algorithm (e.g. Grace- vs. Distributed Block Nested Loop Join vs. Cyclo-Join), the data partitioning of the respective relations, and their overlapping as well as the allowed resource allocation.

We present an evaluation on a cluster with 60 nodes where all nodes are connected via RDMA-enabled network equipment. We show that query processing performance is about 2.4x slower if everything is done via the data pull operator execution strategy (i.e. RAMCloud is being used only for data access) and about 27 % slower if operator execution is also supported inside RAMCloud (in comparison to operating only on main memory inside a server without any network communication at all). The fast-crash recovery feature of RAMCloud can be leveraged to provide high-availability, e.g. a server crash during query execution only delays the query response for about one second. Our solution is elastic in a way that it can adapt to changing workloads (a) within seconds, (b) without interruption of the ongoing query processing, and (c) without manual intervention.

Palo Alto, CA, USA   Christian Tinnefeld
April 2015

Contents

1	**Introduction**		1
	1.1	Motivation	3
	1.2	Research Questions and Scope	4
	1.3	Outline	5
2	**Related Work and Background**		7
	2.1	Current Computing Hardware Trends	7
		2.1.1 Larger and Cheaper Main Memory Capacities	9
		2.1.2 Multi-Core Processors and the Memory Wall	10
		2.1.3 Switch Fabric Network and Remote Direct Memory Access	12
	2.2	In-Memory Database Management Systems	16
		2.2.1 Column- and Row-Oriented Data Layout	17
		2.2.2 Transactional Versus Analytical Versus Mixed Workload Processing	19
		2.2.3 State-of-the-Art In-Memory Database Management Systems	21
	2.3	Parallel Database Management Systems	22
		2.3.1 Shared-Memory Versus Shared-Disk Versus Shared-Nothing	23
		2.3.2 State-of-the-Art Parallel Database Management Systems	26
		2.3.3 Database-Aware Storage Systems	29
		2.3.4 Operator Placement for Distributed Query Processing	30
	2.4	Cloud Storage Systems	34
		2.4.1 State-of-the-Art Cloud Storage Systems	38
		2.4.2 Combining Database Management and Cloud Storage Systems	39
	2.5	Classification	41

**Part I   A Database System Architecture for a Shared
          Main Memory-Based Storage**

3   System Architecture   45
   3.1   System Architecture—Requirements, Assumptions,
      and Overview   45
   3.2   AnalyticsDB   48
   3.3   Stanford's RAMCloud.   50

4   Data Storage   53
   4.1   Mapping from Columnar Data to RAMCloud Objects.   53
   4.2   Main Memory Access Costs and Object Sizing   54

5   Data Processing   63
   5.1   Database Operators in AnalyticsDB   63
   5.2   Operator Push-Down into RAMCloud.   64
   5.3   From SQL Statement to Main Memory Access.   65

**Part II   Database Operator Execution on a Shared
           Main Memory-Based Storage**

6   Operator Execution on One Relation   69
   6.1   Evaluating Operator Execution Strategies.   72
   6.2   Optimizing Operator Execution   75
   6.3   Implications of Data Partitioning   75

7   Operator Execution on Two Relations   79
   7.1   Grace Join.   81
   7.2   Distributed Block Nested Loop Join   83
   7.3   Cyclo Join.   85
   7.4   Join Algorithm Comparison.   87
   7.5   Parallel Join Executions.   90

Part III   Evaluation

8   Performance Evaluation   95
   8.1   Analytical Workload: Star Schema Benchmark.   95
   8.2   Mixed Workload: Point-of-Sales Customer Data.   98

9   High-Availability Evaluation   101

10   Elasticity Evaluation   103

Part IV Conclusions

11 Conclusions 111

Appendix 113

Glossary 115

References.. 119

List of Figures

Figure 2.1   Modified Von Neumann Architecture with added
             system bus   8
Figure 2.2   Memory hierarchy as described by Patterson and
             Hennessy   8
Figure 2.3   Evolution of memory price development and capacity
             per chip advancement [Pla11a, PH08]. Please note that
             both y-axes have a logarithmic scale   9
Figure 2.4   Illustration of the evolution of Intel processors from
             1995 until 2013. **a** Evolution of Intel processor clock
             rate and number of processor cores [Int13]. The figure
             shows that Intel distributed a processor with more than
             3000 Mhz clock rate (Intel Pentium 4Xeon) already in
             2003, but until 2013 the clock rate only evolved to
             3900 Mhz (Intel Core i7 Extreme Edition). The first
             mass-produced processor from Intel with two cores
             (Intel Pentium Dual-Core) came out in 2006: the
             number of cores per processor evolved to twelve in
             2013 (Intel Xeon E5). **b** Comparison of Coremark
             Benchmark Score [The13] and memory bandwidth
             (maximum specified rate at which data can be read
             from or stored to a semiconductor memory by the
             processor) of selected Intel processors [Int13] over
             time. The Coremark benchmark measures the perfor-
             mance of a CPU by executing algorithms such as list
             processing or matrix manipulation and intends to
             replace the Dhrystone [Wei84] benchmark. The figure
             illustrates that the processing power of CPUs increased
             more significantly (by introducing multiple physical
             processing cores per CPU) than its memory
             bandwidth.   11

Figure 2.5   Two different processor interconnect architectures.
               a Shared Front-Side Bus. **b** Intel's Quick Path
               Interconnect   12
Figure 2.6   Comparisons of memory and local area network
               bandwidth and latency specifications from 1995 until
               2013. **a** Comparison of memory and local area network
               bandwidth specifications [HP11, Ass13]. The figure
               illustrates how the bandwidth performance gap narrows
               down from over an order of magnitude (1995: 267
               MBytes/s Fast Page Mode DRAM vs. 12.5 MBytes/s
               Fast Ethernet) to a factor of 1.3 (2010:
               16 GBytes/s DDR3-2000 SDRAM vs. 12.5 GBytes/s
               100 Gigabit Ethernet) over a period of 15 years, and that
               today's local area network technology specifies a higher
               bandwidth than memory (2013: 24 GBytes/s
               DDR3-3000 SDRAM vs. 37.5 GBytes/s Enhanced Data
               Rate (EDR) 12x). **b** Comparison of memory and local
               area network latency specifications [HP11, Ass13]. The
               figure shows that the latency performance gap has been
               reduced from five orders of magnitude (2000: 0.052 µs
               Double Data Rate SDRAM vs. 340 µs Gigabit Ethernet)
               to one to two orders of magnitude (2013: 0.037 µs
               DDR3 SDRAM vs. 1 µs InfiniBand)   14
Figure 2.7   Illustration of a row- and column-oriented data
               layout.   18
Figure 2.8   Comparison of query distribution in analyzed business
               customer systems and a database benchmark (com-
               parison by and figure taken from Krüger et al.
               [KKG⁺11]). The comparison shows that OLTP work-
               loads on customer enterprise resource planning sys-
               tems are also dominated by read operations in contrast
               to the common understanding that OLTP exposes an
               equal mix of read and write operations (as e.g. implied
               by the TPC-C benchmark [Raa93]). **a** Query distribu-
               tion in analyzed business customer systems. **b** Query
               distribution in the TPC-C benchmark   20
Figure 2.9   Three different parallel DBMS architectures.
               a Shared-Memory. **b** Shared-Disk. **c** Shared-Nothing   23
Figure 2.10   Illustration of query, data, and hybrid shipping
               (Figure taken from [Kos00]). **a** Query Shipping.
               b Data Shipping. **c** Hybrid Shipping.   31

Figure 2.11   Depicting the ratio of queries which are eligible for
              query, hybrid or data shipping in correspondence with
              a relational DBMS either acting as server or client.   34
Figure 3.1   Assumptions with regards to the deployed hardware
              and software stacks   46
Figure 3.2   System architecture overview   47
Figure 3.3   AnalyticsDB architecture   49
Figure 3.4   RAMCloud architecture   51
Figure 4.1   Mapping from AnalyticsDB columns to objects in
              RAMCloud. Partitioning of two columns across four
              storage nodes with a server span=3   54
Figure 4.2   Illustration of data region R.   56
Figure 4.3   Single sequential traversal access pattern (taken from
              [MBK02b]).   57
Figure 4.4   Single random traversal access pattern (taken from
              [MBK02b]).   58
Figure 4.5   Single random block traversal access pattern   59
Figure 4.6   Object sizing experiments. **a** Detailed breakdown of
              data traversal with varying block size
              ($Blk.w = \{1, 10, 100, 1000, 10000, 10^6, 10^7\}R.n$,
              b data traversal with varying data item
              ($R.w = \{16, 64, 1024\}Bytes$) and block size
              ($Blk.w = \{1, 4, 8, 16, 128, 1024, 10^7\}R.n$), **c** impact of
              prefetching and block sizing on CPU cycles spent for
              data traversal.   61
Figure 5.1   From SQL statement in AnalyticsDB to the corre-
              sponding main memory access in RAMCloud   66
Figure 6.1   Evaluating operator execution strategies. **a** Scan with
              increasing selectivity. $S_D = 2$, $S_P = 0$, $s = \{0.1 \ldots 1\}$,
              $n = 1$, $BW_{Mem} = 2$ GB/s, **b** Scan with increasing
              number of nodes. $S_D = 2$, $S_P = 0$, $s = 0.5$,
              $n = \{1 \ldots 20\}$, $BW_{Mem} = 2$ GB/s, **c** Materialization
              with increasing position list size. $S_D = 0$,
              $S_P = \{0 \ldots 60 \, \text{Mio.}\}$, $s = 1$, $n = 1$, $BW_{Mem} = 2$ GB/s,
              d Join Probing with increasing probing data size.
              $S_d = \{0 \ldots 60 \, \text{Mio.}\}$, $S_P = 10$ Mio., $s = 0.5$, $N = 20$,
              $BW_{Mem} = 0.4$ GB/s   73
Figure 6.2   Execution of a SQL query on the Star Schema
              Benchmark data set with SF = 1, SC = 6 Mio.,
              Sr = 8 bytes, N = 10 and different execution strate-
              gies. The figure illustrates that for this query a mix of
              data pull and operator push execution strategies is
              preferable   75

Figure 6.3   AnalyticsDB runs on a single node with a operator
              push execution strategy, the RAMCloud cluster has a
              size of 20 nodes, the server span varies   76
Figure 6.4   RAMCloud cluster with a constant number of 20 nodes
              and a varying number (1–30) of nodes running
              AnalyticsDB with a operator push execution strategy
              and a Star Schema Benchmark data scale factor of 10.
              a RAMCloud running on 20 Nodes with Server
              Span=10, **b** RAMCloud running on 20 Nodes with
              Server Span=20.   77
Figure 7.1   Four comparisons of the execution times for different
              join algorithms. Figure 7.1**a, c** are calculations based on
              the system model, Fig. 7.1**b, d** are the respective
              experiments based on the prototypical implementations.
              a Calculation with system model for: $n_{partR/S} = 16$
              nodes, $n_{partOvl} = 16$ nodes, $R_{size} = 1$ GB, $S_{size} = 1$ GB,
              b Experiment with implementation: $n_{partR/S} = 16$ nodes,
              $n_{partOvl} = 16$ nodes, $R_{size} = 1$ GB, $S_{size} = 1$ GB,
              c Calculation with system model for: $n_{partR/S} = 16$
              nodes, $n_{partOvl} = 16$ nodes, $R_{size} = 1$ GB, $S_{size} = 0.1$ GB,
              d Experiment with implementation: $n_{partR/S} = 16$ nodes,
              $n_{partOvl} = 16$ nodes, $R_{size} = 1$ GB, $S_{size} = 0.1$ GB   88
Figure 7.2   Four comparisons of the network transfer and data
              processed in memory for different join algorithms.
              Figure 7.2**a** + **b** depict the network transfer N_{tot},
              Fig. 7.2**c** + **d** illustrate the data amount processed in
              memory J_{tot}. **a** N_{tot} based on the system model for:
              $n_{partR/S} = 16$ nodes, $n_{partOvl} = 16$ nodes, $R_{size} = 1$ GB,
              $S_{size} = 1$ GB, **b** N_{tot} based on the system model for:
              $n_{partR/S} = 16$ nodes, $n_{partOvl} = 16$ nodes, $R_{size} = 1$ GB,
              $S_{size} = 0.1$ GB, **c** J_{tot} based on the system model for:
              $n_{partR/S} = 16$ nodes, $n_{partOvl} = 16$ nodes, $R_{size} = 1$ GB,
              $S_{size} = 1$ GB, **d** J_{tot} based on the system model for:
              $n_{partR/S} = 16$ nodes, $n_{partOvl} = 16$ nodes, $R_{size} = 1$ GB,
              $S_{size} = 0.1$ GB   89
Figure 7.3   Evaluation of join execution heuristics on a cluster
              with 32 nodes and hardware parameters shown in
              Table 7.2   91

Figure 8.1   Operator breakdown for AnalyticsDB executing Star
               Schema Benchmark queries with a data scale factor of
               10 and different storage options and operator execution
               strategies. AnalyticsDB runs on a single node, the
               RAMCloud (RC) cluster has size of 20 nodes. The
               figure illustrates that the data pull execution strategy is
               on average 2.6 times (or 260 %) slower than the
               execution on local DRAM and that the operator push
               execution strategy is on average 11 % slower than the
               execution on local DRAM. **a** Star Schema Benchmark
               Queries 1.1–2.3. **b** Star Schema Benchmark Queries
               3.1–4.3.   96
Figure 8.2   RAMCloud cluster with 20 nodes and a single node
               running AnalyticsDB with a varying Star Schema
               Benchmark data scale factor (SF). The figure shows
               that the ratio between data set size and Star Schema
               Benchmark execution times remain constant with a
               growing data set size. **a** Sizing Factor = 1, **b** Sizing
               Factor = 10, **c** Sizing Factor = 100   97
Figure 8.3   RAMCloud cluster with a varying number of nodes
               and a single node running AnalyticsDB with a operator
               push execution strategy and a Star Schema Benchmark
               data scale factor of 10   97
Figure 8.4   Operator breakdown for executing the customer data
               mixed workload.Operator breakdown for executing the
               point-of-sales customer data mixed workload with
               different operator execution strategies. AnalyticsDB
               runs on a single node, the RAMCloud (RC) cluster has
               a size of 8 nodes. The figure illustrates i.a. that the data
               pull execution strategy is on average 2.2x slower than
               the execution on local DRAM and that the operator
               push execution strategy is on average 44 % slower than
               the execution on local DRAM.   98
Figure 9.1   High-availability experiment with one AnalyticsDB
               and ten RAMCloud nodes. Throughout the experiment
               RAMCloud nodes get killed and the impact on the
               query response time is observed   102
Figure 10.1   Elasticity evaluation with a sinus-shaped workload.
               The number of the nodes in the RAMCloud cluster
               varies depending on the changing workload imposed
               by a changing number of AnalyticsDB nodes. Each
               AnalyticsDB node executes the Star Schema Bench-
               mark at a sizing factor ten, the execution strategy is
               operator push   105

Figure 10.2   Elasticity evaluation with a plateau-shaped workload.
The number of the nodes in the RAMCloud cluster
varies depending on the changing workload imposed
by a changing number of AnalyticsDB nodes. Each
AnalyticsDB node executes the Star Schema Benchmark at a sizing factor ten, the execution strategy is
operator push   106
Figure 10.3   Elasticity evaluation with an quadratically in- and
decreasing workload. The number of the nodes in the
RAMCloud cluster varies in dependence of a changing
workload imposed by a changing number of AnalyticsDB nodes. Each AnalyticsDB node executes the
Star Schema Benchmark at a sizing factor ten, the
execution strategy is operator push.   107

List of Tables

Table 2.1   Bandwidth and latency comparison for accessing local (inside a single computer) and remote (between two separate computers) DRAM 15

Table 2.2   Site selection for different classes of database operators for query, data, and hybrid shipping (Figure taken from [Kos00])................................. 32

Table 4.1   Overview on cache parameters $(i \in \{1, \ldots, N\})^3$ (taken from [MBK02b])............................... 55

Table 5.1   Database Operators in AnalyticsDB 64

Table 5.2   AnalyticsDB operator break-down when executing the Star Schema Benchmark, normalized by the contribution of the operator to the overall query runtime 65

Table 6.1   Symbols in the system model for operating on one relation at a time 71

Table 7.1   System model symbols for operating on two relations at a time....................................... 80

Table 7.2   Hardware parameters 89

Table 7.3   Distribution of join algorithms for Star Schema Benchmark execution as shown in Fig. 7.3 in dependence of the chosen heuristic 91

Table A.1   Star Schema Benchmark relations involved in joins operations. One record has a size of 8 bytes 113

Table A.2   Star Schema Benchmark join operations 114

Chapter 1
Introduction

Elmasri and Navathe [EN10] describe a database system as consisting of a database and a database management system (DBMS). They define a database as "a collection of related data" and a DBMS as "a collection of programs that enables users to create and maintain a database. The DBMS is hence a general-purpose software system that facilitates the process of defining, constructing, manipulating, and sharing databases among various users and applications". According to Hellerstein and Stonebraker [HS05], IBM DB/2 [HS13], PostgreSQL [Sto87], and Sybase SQL Server [Kir96] are typical representatives of database management systems. These DBMSs are optimized for the characteristics of disk storage mechanisms. In their seminal paper *Main Memory Database Systems: An Overview* [GMS92] from 1992, Garcia-Molina and Salem describe a main memory database system[1] (MMDB) as a database system where data "resides permanently in main physical memory". Operating on data that resides in main memory results in an order of magnitude better performance than operating on data that sits on a disk. In the last century, main memory database systems played only a minor role in the overall database market as the capacities of main memory chips were small yet very expensive. This development changed significantly in the last decade, resulting in main memory database systems becoming more popular: for example Plattner [Pla09, Pla11a] presents SanssouciDB as a main memory DBMS that is tailored for supporting the execution of modern business applications.

Since the storage capacity and processing power of a single server is limited, one motivation for deploying a distributed database system is the combination of the hardware resources provided by many servers. Özsu and Valduriez [ÖV11] define a distributed database as

> a collection of multiple, logically interrelated databases distributed over a computer network. A distributed database management system is then defined as the software system that permits the management of the distributed database system and makes the distribution transparent to the users.

---

[1]Throughout this work, the terms *main memory database system* and *in-memory database system* are being used interchangeably.

© Springer International Publishing Switzerland 2016
C. Tinnefeld, *Building a Columnar Database on RAMCloud*, In-Memory
Data Management Research, DOI 10.1007/978-3-319-20711-7_1

with a DBMS. However, the motivation is to find out how close the aforementioned external factors bring such a system to the ideal, and if they have the potential to end the one-sidedness of the architectural landscape for parallel main memory database systems which is currently dominated by the shared-nothing approach.

On the other hand, there are a range of applications which would benefit from a main memory parallel DBMS based on a shared-storage architecture. Two examples are:

- **Cold Store**: Garcia-Molina and Salem [GMS92] argue that it is reasonable to assume that the entire database of some applications can fit into main memory. For those applications where this is not the case, a hot and cold data partitioning schema is being proposed: frequently queried, fast accessible data which is usually of low volume is being kept in main memory (hot store), whereas rarely accessed more voluminous data can be stored on a slower storage medium (cold store). The different data partitions can be realized for example by having several logical databases. With the advent of a storage system that keeps all data resident in main memory, it seems beneficial to use it as shared-storage for the DBMS that serves the cold data. The performance characteristics for accessing this data may not be as good as operating on local main memory inside a server, but the real challenge for a cold store is scaling out gracefully as the amount of cold data grows over time and the required storage capacity increases.
- **On-Demand In-Memory Computing**: nowadays information technology infra-structure, services and applications can be provisioned over the Internet. Typical characteristics are the on-demand availability of these resources, their quick adaption to changing workloads, and the billing based on actual usage. These offerings include the provisioning of an in-memory database such as the availability of SAP's in-memory database HANA hosted at Amazon Web Services [Ser13]. Solutions exist to adapt the capacity of an in-memory database that is based on a shared-nothing architecture to fluctuating workloads, as summarized and extended by the work of Schaffner et al. [Sch13, SJK+13]. However, utilizing a shared-storage architecture for providing on-demand in-memory computing bears the advantages that a) storage and processing capacities can be adjusted independently, and b) that the complexity of the DBMS software can be reduced as mechanisms such as data redistribution in case of a scale-out are implemented and hidden in the storage system.

1.2 Research Questions and Scope

This work focuses on the implications of building a columnar database on a shared main memory-based storage and the resulting database operator placement problem in a shared main memory-based storage system that supports data access and code execution. This leads to the following research questions:

1. What is a suitable architecture for a main memory database in order to utilize a shared main memory-based storage?
2. Where to place the execution of a database operator (site selection) in a main memory-based storage system that supports data access and code execution (data-pull versus operator-push)?
3. What is the performance penalty for the execution of database operators not on the local main memory inside a server, but on a remote main memory over a RDMA-enabled network?
4. Can the fast-recovery mechanism provided by a modern, main memory-based storage system be leveraged by a database application, so that a hardware failure does not interrupt query processing?
5. Can the elasticity provided by a modern, main memory-based storage system that is incorporated in shared-storage parallel DBMS be leveraged to maintain a constant query execution time under a varying workload?

While the aforementioned research questions span the scope of this work, the following aspects are considered out of scope:

• This work does not aim to compare different parallel DBMS architectures, let alone to try to come up with a verdict, which one is superior. As presented in Chap. 2, this is a much discussed and long debated aspect of parallel DBMSs and—as discussed in Sect. 2.3.1—work already exists that solely addresses architectural comparisons.
• This work does not consider distributed transaction processing. The aspect of distributed transaction processing in the context of query execution, in conjunction with a modern main memory-based storage system, is currently under research at the ETH Zürich [SG13]. As described in Sect. 3.2, we assume that there is a single, central instance that handles all write operations.
• This work does not dive into the details or present a comparison of different high-end network technologies. This work describes the concepts behind RDMA-enabled network technology in Sect. 2.1.3, and takes it for the remainder as granted.

1.3 Outline

The book is divided into three parts preceded by this introduction and the presentation of related work and background in Chap. 2. Chapter 2 explains the four major areas influencing this work: current computing hardware trends in Sect. 2.1, in-memory database management systems in Sect. 2.2, parallel database management systems in Sect. 2.3, and cloud storage systems in Sect. 2.4. The description of the related work closes with a classification in Sect. 2.5.

Part I presents a database system architecture for a shared main memory-based storage and consists of three chapters. Chapter 3 describes the architectural requirements and assumptions, presents an overview and introduces the components AnalyticsDB and RAMCloud. Chapter 4 deals with the resulting data storage implications and illustrates how columnar data inside AnalyticsDB is mapped to objects in RAMCloud, and how the right sizing of these objects can uphold the advantages of a columnar data layout. Chapter 5 illustrates the data processing by describing the database operators in AnalyticsDB and how to push their execution into RAMCloud.

Part II tackles the site selection problem in detail and presents a study of database operator execution on a shared main memory-based storage. Chapter 6 explains the operator execution on one relation at a time, presents the related system model in detail, evaluates the different operator execution strategies, illustrates the subsequent optimization of a query execution and points out the implications of data partitioning. Chapter 7 extends the system model to describe the costs for the execution of an operator that works on two relations, such as the distributed join algorithms Grace Join, Distributed Block Nested Loop Join and Cyclo Join. The chapter continues with a comparison of these algorithms and the influence of partitioning criteria and resource allocation on their parallel executions.

Part III presents an evaluation of our system with regards to performance, high-availability, and elasticity. Chapter 8 presents a performance evaluation that aims to quantify the gap between query execution on local and remote main memory while considering the different operator execution strategies (data pull versus operator push). Two different workloads are being used: an analytical workload consisting of the Star Schema Benchmark, and a mixed workload based on point-of-sales customer data from a large European retailer. Chapter 9 evaluates the high-availability of our solution by provoking server crashes during query execution. Chapter 10 evaluates the elasticity by aiming to maintain a constant query processing time under a heavily varying workload. Chapter 11 closes with the conclusions.

Chapter 2
Related Work and Background

This chapter presents the background as well as the related work for this work. Instead of separating the chapters *related work* and *background*, both topics are presented together in one chapter, giving the reader the advantage of understanding underlying concepts and getting to know the respective related work in one stroke. Each section and subsection is preceded by a short summary. Additional related work is presented where appropriate for example Chap. 6 starts with discussing system models which are related to the system model presented in remainder of this chapter, while Chap. 7 contains an overview on state-of-the-art distributed join algorithms. The four major areas which influence this work are current computing hardware trends, in-memory database management systems, parallel database management systems, as well as cloud storage systems. The subsequent sections and subsections also include discussions regarding how the different areas influence each other.

2.1 Current Computing Hardware Trends

Summary: This section introduces the computing hardware trends by describing the foundation for current computer architecture.

John Von Neumann described in 1945 [vN93] a computer architecture that consists of the following basic components: (a) an Arithmetic Logic Unit (ALU), also known as processor which executes calculations and logical operations; (b) memory which holds a program and its to be processed data; (c) a Control Unit that moves program and data into and out of the memory and executes the program instructions. For supporting the execution of the instructions the Control Unit can use a Register for storing intermediate values; (d) an Input and Output mechanism allows the interaction with external entities such as a user via keyboard and screen. The original Von Neumann architecture included the interconnection of the different architectural components, however an explicit System Bus has been added later to be able to connect a non-volatile memory medium for persistent data storage [NL06]. Figure 2.1 depicts the Von Neumann Architecture with an added system bus.

© Springer International Publishing Switzerland 2016　　　　　　　　　　7
C. Tinnefeld, *Building a Columnar Database on RAMCloud*, In-Memory
Data Management Research, DOI 10.1007/978-3-319-20711-7_2

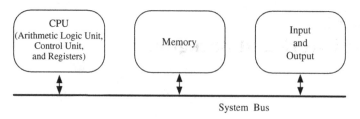

Fig. 2.1 Modified Von Neumann Architecture with added system bus

As indicated in the description of the Von Neumann architecture, there are different types of memory technologies which vary in properties such as cost ($ per bit), access performance, and volatility. Inside a single computer, a combination of different memory technologies is used with the intention of combining their advantages. The combination of the different technologies is done by aligning them in a hierarchy in order to create the illusion that the overall memory is as large as the largest level of the hierarchy. Such a memory hierarchy can be composed of multiple levels and data is transferred between two adjacent levels at a time. As shown in Fig. 2.2, the upper levels are usually smaller, faster, more expensive, and closer to the CPU, whereas the lower levels provide more capacity (due to the lower costs), but are slower in terms of access performance. The textbook memory technology examples from Patterson and Hennessy [PH08] are SRAM (static random access memory), DRAM (dynamic random access memory), and magnetic disk which build a three-level hierarchy: SRAM provides fast access times, but requires more transistors for storing a single bit which makes it expensive and taking up more space [HP11]. SRAM is used in today's computers as a cache very close to the CPU and is the first memory level in this example. DRAM is less costly per bit than SRAM, but also substantially slower and is the second memory level and is used as main memory for holding currently processed data and programs. In addition, DRAM cells need

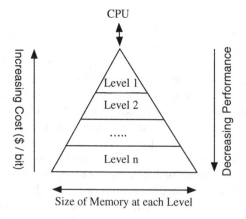

Fig. 2.2 Memory hierarchy as described by Patterson and Hennessy

constant energy supply otherwise they loose the stored information which makes them volatile. In order to permanently store data, a third memory hierarchy is introduced that uses a magnetic disk. However, the moving parts inside a magnetic disk result in a penalty with regards to the access performance in comparison to DRAM. Two other frequently used terms for differentiating between volatile and non-volatile memory are primary and secondary memory [PH08]: primary memory is a synonym for volatile memory such as main memory holding currently processed programs and data, whereas secondary memory is non-volatile memory storing programs and data between runs. A shortcoming of the Von Neumann Architecture is that the CPU can either read an instruction or data from memory at the same time. This is addressed by the Harvard architecture [HP11] which physically separates storage and signal pathways for instructions and data.

Reflecting on the Von Neumann Architecture and the aspect of memory hierarchies, it becomes apparent that a computer is a combination of different hardware components with unique properties and that the capabilities of those hardware components ultimately set the boundaries of the capabilities of the to-be-run programs on that computer. Consequently, hardware trends also impact the way computer programs are designed and utilize the underlying hardware. In the remainder of this section we want to describe three hardware trends which contribute to the motivation for this work.

2.1.1 Larger and Cheaper Main Memory Capacities

Summary: This subsection quantifies the advancements in main memory capacities and the price reduction over the last 18 years.

The price for main memory DRAM modules has dropped constantly during the previous years. As shown in Fig. 2.3, the price for one megabyte of main memory

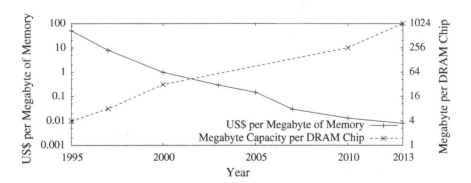

Fig. 2.3 Evolution of memory price development and capacity per chip advancement [Pla11a, PH08]. Please note that both y-axes have a logarithmic scale

used to be \$50 in 1995, and dropped to \$0.03 in 2007—a price reduction of three orders of magnitudes in about 20 years. In addition, chip manufacturers managed to pack transistors and capacitors more densely, which increased the capacity per chip. In 1995, a single DRAM chip had the capacity of 4 Megabytes, which increased to 1024 Megabyte per chip in 2013. Putting 32 of those chips on a single DRAM module gives it a capacity of 32 Gigabytes. Nowadays, server mainboards (e.g. Intel[1] Server Board S4600LH2 [Int13]) can hold up to 48 of those modules, resulting in a capacity of 1.5 terabyte of main memory per board. Such an Intel server board equipped with 1.5 terabyte of Kingston server-grade memory can be bought for under \$25,000 (undiscounted retail price [new13]), which illustrates the combination of price decline and advancement in capacity per chip.

Despite the previously described developments, solid-state drives (SSD) and hard-disk drives (HDD) still have a more attractive price point—e.g. the cost per megabyte capacity of a three terabyte hard-disk is about \$0.004 [new13]. In addition, DRAM is a volatile storage and as long as non-volatile memory is not being mass-produced, one always needs the same capacity of SSD/HDD storage somewhere to durably store the data being kept and processed in DRAM (the situation is comparable to alternative energy sources—you still need the coal power plant when the sun is not shining or the wind is not blowing). However, in the end the performance advantage of operating on main memory outweighs the higher cost per megabyte in the context of performance critical applications such as large-scale web applications [mem13a] or in-memory databases [Pla11a].

2.1.2 Multi-Core Processors and the Memory Wall

Summary: This subsection describes the development of having multiple cores per processor and the resulting main memory access bottleneck.

In 1965, Gordon Moore made a statement about the future development of the complexity of integrated circuits in the semiconductor industry [Moo65]. His prediction that the number of transistors on a single chip is doubled approximately every two years became famous as Moore's Law, as it turned out to be a relatively accurate prediction.

The development of the processors clock rate and the number of processor cores is of relevance: as depicted in Fig. 2.4a, Intel CPUs reached a clock rate of 3000 Mhz in 2003. Until then the clock rate improved from yearly which used to be convenient for a programmer, as he usually did not have to adjust his code in order to leverage the capabilities of a new generation of processors. This changed for Intel processors between 2003 and 2006, when a further increasement of the clock rate would have

---

[1] There is a great variety of computer processor and mainboard vendors such as AMD [AMD13], GIGABYTE [GIG13] or Intel [Int13]. For the sake of better comparability throughout the different subsections, this section cites only Intel processor and mainboard products. In addition, Intel holds a market share of over 90 % in the worldwide server processor market in 2012 [RS13].

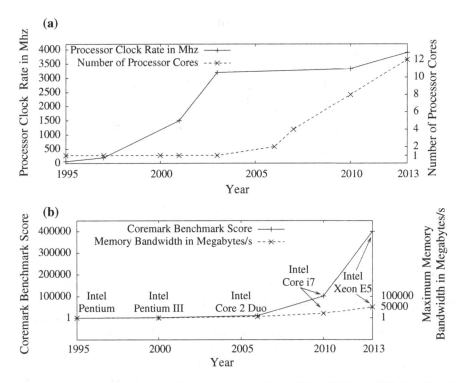

Fig. 2.4 Illustration of the evolution of Intel processors from 1995 until 2013. **a** Evolution of Intel processor clock rate and number of processor cores [Int13]. The figure shows that Intel distributed a processor with more than 3000 Mhz clock rate (Intel Pentium 4 Xeon) already in 2003, but until 2013 the clock rate only evolved to 3900 Mhz (Intel Core i7 Extreme Edition). The first mass-produced processor from Intel with two cores (Intel Pentium Dual-Core) came out in 2006: the number of cores per processor evolved to twelve in 2013 (Intel Xeon E5). **b** Comparison of Coremark Benchmark Score [The13] and memory bandwidth (maximum specified rate at which data can be read from or stored to a semiconductor memory by the processor) of selected Intel processors [Int13] over time. The Coremark benchmark measures the performance of a CPU by executing algorithms such as list processing or matrix manipulation and intends to replace the Dhrystone [Wei84] benchmark. The figure illustrates that the processing power of CPUs increased more significantly (by introducing multiple physical processing cores per CPU) than its memory bandwidth

resulted in too much power consumption and heat emission. Instead, the clock rate remained relatively stable, but having more than one physical processing core per (multi-core) CPU was introduced. This led to the saying that the *free lunch is over* [Sut05], now application developers had to write their software accordingly to utilize the capabilities of multi-core CPUs. This is also expressed by Amdahl's Law, which says that the speed up of a system can also be defined as the fraction of code that can be parallelized [Amd67]. Reflecting on the importance of main memory as mentioned in the previous subsection, Fig. 2.4b shows the development of CPU processing power and its memory bandwidth. One can observe that with the advent of multiple cores

(a)   **(b)**

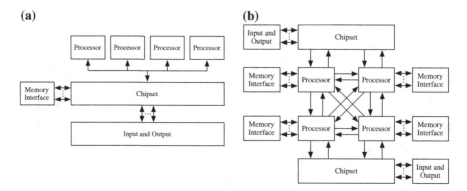

Fig. 2.5 Two different processor interconnect architectures. **a** Shared Front-Side Bus. **b** Intel's Quick Path Interconnect

per processor, processing power spiked significantly: an equivalent increase in the maximum specified rate at which data can be read from or stored into a semiconductor memory by the processor could not be realized [BGK96].

As described in the beginning of this section, a processor is not directly wired to the main memory, but accesses it over a system bus. This system bus becomes a bottle neck when multiple processors or processor cores utilize it. Figure 2.5a shows a shared front-side bus architecture where several processors access the memory over a shared bus. Here, the access time to data in memory is independent regardless which processor makes the request or which memory chip contains the transferred data: this is called uniform memory access (UMA). In order to overcome the bottleneck of having a single shared bus, for example, Intel introduced Quick Path Interconnect as depicted in Fig. 2.5b, where every processor has its exclusively assigned memory. In addition, each processor is directly interconnected with each other, which increases the overall bandwidth between the different processors and the memory. A single processor can access its local memory or the memory of another processor, whereat the memory access time depends on the memory location relative to the processor. Therefore, such an architecture is described as NUMA, standing for non-uniform memory access.

2.1.3 Switch Fabric Network and Remote Direct Memory Access

Summary: This subsection quantifies the advancements of network bandwidth and latency over the last 18 years, as well as the closing performance gap between accessing main memory inside a server and that of a remote server.

The previous subsection describes the performance characteristics when operating on the main memory inside a single server. Although Sect. 2.1.1 emphasizes the

growing main memory capacities inside a single server, the storage space requirements from an application can exceed this capacity. When utilizing the main memory
capacities from several servers, the performance characteristics from the network
interconnect between the servers have to be considered as well. Modern network
technologies such as InfiniBand or Ethernet Fabrics have a switched fabric topology
which means that (a) each network node connects with each other via one or more
switches and (b) that the connection between two nodes is established based on the
crossbar switch theory [Mat01] resulting in no resource conflicts with connections
between any other nodes at the same time [GS02]: in the case of InfiniBand, this
results in full bisection bandwidth between any two nodes at any time. In addition the
InfiniBand specification [Ass13] describes that an InfiniBand link can be operated
at five different data rates: 0.25 GBytes/s for single data rate (SDR), 0.5 GBytes/s
for double data rate, 1 GBytes/s for quad data rate (QDR), 1.7 GBytes/s for fourteen
data rate (FDR), and 3.125 GBytes/s for enhanced data rate (EDR). In addition, an
InfiniBand connection between two devices can aggregate several links in units of
four and twelve (typically denoted as 4x or 12x). For example, the aggregation of four
quad data rate links results in 4xQDR with a specified data rate of 4 GBytes/s. These
specifications describe the effective theoretical unidirectional throughput, meaning
that the overall bandwidth between two hosts can be twice as high.

Figure 2.6a compares the bandwidth specifications of main memory and network
technologies. The figure shows how the bandwidth performance gap narrows down
from over an order of magnitude (1995: 267 MBytes/s Fast Page Mode DRAM
versus 12.5 MBytes/s Fast Ethernet) to a factor of 1.3 (2010: 16 GBytes/s DDR3-
2000 SDRAM versus 12.5 GBytes/s 100 Gigabit Ethernet) over a period of 15 years,
and that today's local area network technology specifies a higher bandwidth than
memory (2013: 24 GBytes/s DDR3-3000 SDRAM versus 37.5 GBytes/s InfiniBand
Enhanced Data Rate (EDR) 12x). Figure 2.6b compares the latency specifications of
main memory and network technologies. The figure depicts how the latency performance gap has been reduced from five orders of magnitude (2000: 0.052 μs Double
Data Rate SDRAM versus 340 μs Gigabit Ethernet) to two orders of magnitude
(2013: 0.037 μs DDR3 SDRAM vs 1 μs InfiniBand). The recent improvement in
network latency is the result of applying a technique called remote direct memory
access (RDMA). RDMA enables the network interface card to transfer data directly
into the main memory which bypasses the operating system by eliminating the need
to copy data into the data buffers in the operating system (which is also known as zero-
copy networking)—which in turn also increases the available bandwidth. In addition,
transferring data via RDMA can be done without invoking the CPU [Mel13]. RDMA
was originally intended to be used in the context of high-performance computing and
is currently implemented in networking hardware such as InfiniBand. However, three
trends indicate that RDMA can become wide-spread in the context of standardized
computer server hardware: From a specification perspective, RDMA over Converged
Ethernet (RoCE) allows remote direct memory access over an Ethernet network and
network interface cards supporting RoCE are available on the market. From an operating system perspective, for example Microsoft supports RDMA in Windows 8
and Windows Server 2012 [WW13]. From a hardware perspective, it is likely that

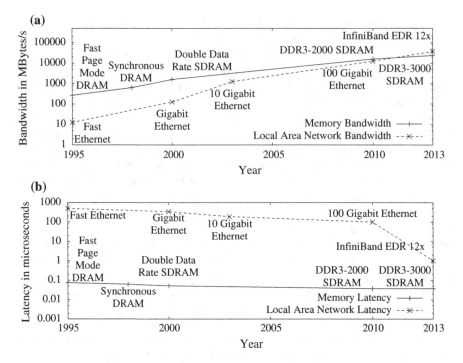

Fig. 2.6 Comparisons of memory and local area network bandwidth and latency specifications from 1995 until 2013. **a** Comparison of memory and local area network bandwidth specifications [HP11, Ass13]. The figure illustrates how the bandwidth performance gap narrows down from over an order of magnitude (1995: 267 MBytes/s Fast Page Mode DRAM vs. 12.5 MBytes/s Fast Ethernet) to a factor of 1.3 (2010: 16 GBytes/s DDR3-2000 SDRAM vs. 12.5 GBytes/s 100 Gigabit Ethernet) over a period of 15 years, and that today's local area network technology specifies a higher bandwidth than memory (2013: 24 GBytes/s DDR3-3000 SDRAM vs. 37.5 GBytes/s Enhanced Data Rate (EDR) 12x). **b** Comparison of memory and local area network latency specifications [HP11, Ass13]. The figure shows that the latency performance gap has been reduced from five orders of magnitude (2000: 0.052 μs Double Data Rate SDRAM vs. 340 μs Gigabit Ethernet) to one to two orders of magnitude (2013: 0.037 μs DDR3 SDRAM vs. 1 μs InfiniBand)

RDMA capable network controller chips become on-board commodity equipment on server-grade mainboards.

The comparison of main memory and network technology specifications suggest that the performance gap between operating on local (inside a single computer) and remote (between two separate computers) memory closes. Table 2.1 presents a comparison of hardware specifications and actual measurements in order to quantify the bandwidth and latency performance gap between main memory and network technologies. The Intel Nehalem architecture—which is going to be used in the context of the measurements—specifies a maximum bandwidth of 32 GBytes/s by combining its three memory channels per processor [Tho11]. The specified access latency for retrieving a single cache line from main memory that is not resident in the caches

Table 2.1 Bandwidth and latency comparison for accessing local (inside a single computer) and remote (between two separate computers) DRAM

	Specification		Measurements[3]	
	Intel Nehalem[Tho11] Specification	InfiniBand[Ass13] Specification 4xFDR/12xEDR	Intel Xeon Processor E5-4650	Mellanox ConnectX-3 4xFDR
Bandwidth	32 GBytes/s[1] Memory Bandwidth	6.75 GBytes/s[2] 37.5 GBytes/s[2]	10.2 GBytes/s[4] Memory Bandwidth	4.7 GBytes/s[6]
Latency	0.06 μs Uncached Main Memory Access	1 μs RDMA Operation End-to-End Latency	0.07 μs[5] Uncached Main Memory Access	1.87 μs[6] RDMA Operation End-to-End Latency

[1]Combined memory bandwidth of three memory channels per processor
[2]These are the specified actual data rates (not signaling rates) for 4xFDR respective 12xEDR
[3]Measurements have been performed on the following hardware: Intel Xeon E5-4650 CPU, 24GB DDR3 DRAM, Mellanox ConnectX-3 MCX354A-FCBT 4xFDR InfiniBand NIC connected via Mellanox InfiniScale IV switch
[5]Measured via Bandwidth Benchmark from Z. Smith [Smil13]—Sequential read of 64MB sized objects
[4]Measured via Cache-Memory and TLB Calibration Tool from S. Manegold and S. Boncz [MDK02a]
[6]Measured via native *InfiniBand Open Fabrics Enterprise Distribution* benchmarking tools *ib_read_bw* and *ib_read_lat*

between the CPU and the main memory is 0.06 μs. Actual measurements with an Intel Xeon E5-4650 processor show a memory bandwidth of 10.2 GBytes/s and a memory access latency of 0.07 μs. The difference between the bandwidth specification and the measurement is the number of memory channels: the memory traversal of a data region executed by a single processor core usually invokes a single memory channel at a time, resulting in approximately one third of the specified bandwidth (due to the three available memory channels). Current typical InfiniBand equipment, such as Mellanox ConnectX-3 cards (e.g. Mellanox ConnectX-3 MCX354A-FCBT), support 4xFDR, resulting in a unidirectional data rate of 6.75 GBytes/s between two devises (as previously mentioned, the current InfiniBand specification [Ass13] itself supports up to 37.5 GBytes/s (12xEDR)). The end-to-end latency for a RDMA operation is specified with 1 μs. Measurements between two machines, each equipped with a Mellanox ConnectX-3 MCX354A-FCBT card and connected via a Mellanox InfiniScale IV switch, reveal a unidirectional bandwidth of 4.7 GBytes/s and an end-to-end latency for a RDMA operation of 1.87 μs. The comparison of the measurement results requires a certain carefulness, as it is debatable what is the correct way and appropriate granularity to compare the local and the remote bandwidth: should a single or several combined memory channels be cited, a single InfiniBand link or the aggregation of multiple links, and would one quote the unidirectional or bidirectional bandwidth between two machines? Ultimately, the comparison of the measurements intends to illustrate the ballpark performance gap that can be summarized as follows: as shown in Fig. 2.6, from a bandwidth perspective, local and remote memory access are in the same order of magnitude, and depending on the chosen performance metric, even on par. When it comes to comparing the latency of main memory access inside a machine and between two separate machines, there is still a gap of one to two orders of magnitude.

2.2 In-Memory Database Management Systems

Summary: This section describes a database management system where the data permanently resides in physical main memory.
As mentioned in Chap. 1, Elmasri and Navathe [EN10] describe a database system as consisting of a database and a database management system (DBMS). They define a database as "a collection of related data" and a DBMS as "a collection of programs that enables users to create and maintain a database. The DBMS is hence a general-purpose software system that facilitates the process of defining, constructing, manipulating, and sharing databases among various users and applications". According to Hellerstein and Stonebraker [HS05], IBM DB/2 [HS13], PostgreSQL [Sto87], and Sybase SQL Server [Kir96] are typical representatives of relational database management systems. The term *relational* in the context of the aforementioned DBMSs refers to the implementation of the relational data model by Codd [Cod70], which allows querying the database by using a Structured (English) Query Language initially abbreviated as SEQUEL then shortened to SQL [CB74]. This led to the SQL-standard which is regularly updated [Zem12] and is ISO-certified. Usually a SQL query is issued by an application to a DBMS. The DBMS then parses the query and creates a query plan potentially with the help of a query optimizer. The query plan is then executed by a query execution engine which orchestrates a set of database operators (such as a scan or join) in order to create the result for that query [GMUW08].

The previously mentioned DBMSs are optimized for the characteristics of disk storage mechanisms. In their paper *Main Memory Database Systems: An Overview* [GMS92] from 1992, Garcia-Molina and Salem describe a main memory database system (MMDB) as a database system where data "resides permanently in main physical memory". They argue that in a disk-based DBMS the data is cached in main memory for access, where in a main memory database system the permanently in memory residing data may have a backup copy on disk. They observe that in both cases a data item can have copies in memory and on disk at the same time. However, they also note the following main difference when it comes to accessing data that resides in main memory:

1. The access time for main memory is orders of magnitude less than for disk storage.
2. Main memory is normally volatile, while disk storage is not. However it is possible (at some cost) to construct nonvolatile memory.
3. Disks have a high, fixed cost per access that does not depend on the amount of data that is retrieved during the access. For this reason, disks are block-oriented storage devices. Main memory is not block oriented.
4. The layout of data on a disk is much more critical than the layout of data in main memory, since sequential access to a disk is faster than random access. Sequential access is not as important in main memories.
5. Main memory is normally directly accessible by the processor(s), while disks are not. This may make data in main memory more vulnerable than disk resident data to software errors. [GMS92]

In the remainder of their paper, Garcia-Molina and Salem describe the implications of memory resident data on database system design aspects such as access methods (e.g. index structures do not need to hold a copy of the indexed data, but just a pointer), query processing (e.g. focus should be on processing costs rather than minimize disk access) or recovery (e.g. use of checkpointing to and recovery from disk). IBM's Office-By-Example [AHK85], IMS/VS Fast Path [GK85] or System M from Princeton [SGM90] are presented as state-of-the-art main memory database systems at that time. The further development of memory technology in the subsequent 20 years after this statement—as illustrated in detail in Sect. 2.1.1 and Fig. 2.3—led to increased interest in main memory databases. Plattner describes in 2011 [Pla11a,Pla11b] an in-memory database system called SanssouciDB which is tailored for business applications. SanssouciDB takes hardware developments such as multi-core processors and the resulting importance of the memory wall—as explained in Sect. 2.1.2—into consideration and leverages them by allowing inter- and intra-query parallelism and exploiting cache hierarchies: an important enabler for this is the use of a columnar data layout which will be discussed in detail in the next two subsections.

2.2.1 Column- and Row-Oriented Data Layout

Summary: This subsection distinguishes between two physical database table layouts, namely storing all tuples of a record together (row-orientation) or storing all instances of the same attribute type from different tuples together (column-orientation).

As quoted in the previous subsection, Garcia-Molina and Salem [GMS92] stated that "sequential access is not as important in main memories" in comparison to disk-resident data. While the performance penalty for non-sequential data traversal is higher when operating on disk, it is also exists when accessing data that is in main memory. As described in Sect. 2.1 and as evaluated by Ailamaki et al. [ADHW99] or Boncz, Manegold, and Kersten [BMK99], the access latency from the processor to data in main memory is not truly random due to the memory hierarchy. Since the data travels from main memory through the caches to the processor, it is of relevance if all the data that sits on a cache line is truly being used (cache locality) by the processor and if a requested cache line is already present in one of the caches (temporal locality). In addition, a sequential traversal of data is a pattern that modern CPUs can detect and improve the traversal performance by loading the next to be accessed cache line while the previous cache line is still being processed: this mechanism is known as hardware prefetching (spatial locality) [HP11].

If these mechanisms can be exploited depends on the chosen data layout and the kind of data access thereupon. The two basic distinctions for a data layout are the n-ary storage model (NSM) and the decomposed storage model[CK85]. In NSM, all attributes of a tuple are physically stored together, whereas in DSM the instances of the same attribute type from different tuples are stored together. In database table terms, NSM is declared as a row-oriented data layout and DSM is called a column-

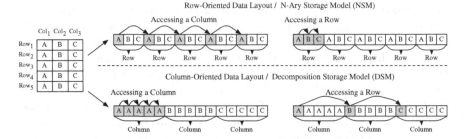

Fig. 2.7 Illustration of a row- and column-oriented data layout

oriented layout. As shown in Fig. 2.7, accessing a row or accessing a column can both leverage the benefits of locality if the data layout has been chosen accordingly. This has led to the classic distinction that databases which are intended for workloads that center around transaction processing and operate on a few rows at a time choose a row-oriented layout and read-only workloads that scan over table attributes and therefore operate on columns choose a column-oriented layout [AMH08]—the next subsection is going to discuss the classification of workloads in detail.

Another aspect in the discussion of row- and column-oriented data layout is that light weight data compression mechanisms work particularly well in a columnar data layout [AMF06]. The intention for using compression mechanisms is saving storage space and—by traversing fewer bytes for processing the same amount of information—increasing performance. The term *light-weight* describes the compression on a sequence of values (e.g. in contrast to heavy weight which refers to the compression of an array of bytes) with techniques such as dictionary compression, run-length encoding (RLE), and bit-vector encoding: these mechanisms allow the processing of a query on the compressed values and it is desirable to decompress the values as late as possible—for example, before returning the result of a query to the user. Dictionary compression is appealing in a columnar data layout as the values inside a single column have the same data type and similar semantics (in contrast to the data inside a single row). The resulting low entropy inside a column can be exploited by dictionary compression in order to reduce the required storage space drastically. Additionally, bit-vector encoding can be used to further reduce the needed storage space: e.g. if a column has up to 4096 different values in total, it can be encoded with a dictionary key size of 12 bit, and the first 60 bits of an 8-byte integer can hold five different column values. Run-length encoding can be applied to columns if they contain sequences in which the same data value occurs multiple times: instead of storing each occurrence separately, RLE allows storing the value once accompanied by the number of subsequent occurrences.

2.2.2 Transactional Versus Analytical Versus Mixed Workload Processing

Summary: This subsection explains different database workloads and how they are being affected by the choice of the data layout.

As implied in the previous subsection, database textbooks contain a distinction between online transaction processing (OLTP) and online analytical processing (OLAP) [EN10]. The term *online* expresses the instant processing of a query and delivering its result. The term *transaction* in OLTP refers to a database transaction which, in turn, has been named after the concept of a business or commercial transaction. Typical examples for OLTP applications are bank teller processing, airline reservation processing or insurance claims processing [BN97]. OLTP workloads are characterized by operating on a few rows per query with an equal mix of read and write operations. The term *analytical* in OLAP describes the intent to perform analysis on data. These analyses consist of ad-hoc queries which for example are issued to support a decision. Systems that are designed for handling OLAP workloads are also referred to as decision support systems (DSS) [Tur90]. An OLAP workload is characterized by executing aggregations over the values of a database table issued by read-mostly queries [Tho02]. OLTP and OLAP work on semantically the same data (e.g. sales transactions are recorded by an OLTP system and then analyzed with an OLAP system), yet they are typically separate systems. Initially, analytical queries were executed against the transactional system, but at the beginning of the 1990s large corporations were no longer able to do so as the performance of the transactional system was not good enough for handling both workloads at the same time. This led to the introduction of OLAP and the separation of the two systems [CCS93]. However, the resulting duplication and separation of data introduced a series of drawbacks. First, the duplication and transformation of data from the transactional to the analytical system (known as extract, transform, and load (ETL) [KC04]) requires additional processing for data denormalization and rearranging. Second, since the execution of the ETL procedure happens only periodically (e.g. once a day), the analytical processing happens on slightly outdated data. Third, the provisioning of a dedicated system for analytical processing requires additional resources.

As a consequence, there are two motivational factors for a reunification of OLTP and OLAP systems as proposed by Plattner [Pla09]: First, the elimination of the previously explained drawbacks resulting from the separation and second, the support of applications which cannot be clearly assigned to one of the workload categories, but expose a mix of many analytical queries and some transactional queries. Tinnefeld et al. [Tin09, KTGP10] elaborate that especially business applications, such as the available-to-promise (ATP) application [TMK+11], expose a mixed workload. An ATP application evaluates if a requested quantity of a product can be delivered to a customer at a requested date. This is done by aggregating and evaluating stock levels and to-be-produced goods with analytical queries, followed by transactional queries upon the reservation of products by the customer.

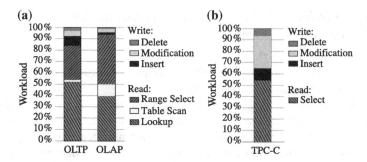

Fig. 2.8 Comparison of query distribution in analyzed business customer systems and a database benchmark (comparison by and figure taken from Krüger et al. [KKG⁺11]). The comparison shows that OLTP workloads on customer enterprise resource planning systems are also dominated by read operations in contrast to the common understanding that OLTP exposes an equal mix of read and write operations (as e.g. implied by the TPC-C benchmark [Raa93]). **a** Query distribution in analyzed business customer systems. **b** Query distribution in the TPC-C benchmark

In order to find a common database approach for OLTP and OLAP, it is logical to reevaluate if the previously mentioned workload characterizations are accurate [Pla09]. Krüger et al. [KKG⁺11] evaluated the query processing in twelve enterprise resource planning (ERP) systems from medium- and large-sized companies with an average of 74,000 database tables per customer system. As shown in Fig. 2.8a, the distribution of queries in the OLAP category is as expected: over 90 % of the queries are read operations dominated by range select operations. The OLTP queries, however, also consist of over 80 % read queries dominated by lookup operations. Only 17 % of the overall queries result in write operations: a contradiction to the common understanding that OLTP consists of an equal mix of read and write queries. This misconception can be visualized by looking at the query distribution of the TPC-C benchmark (which is the standard benchmark for OLTP systems [Raa93]) as shown in Fig. 2.8b: almost 50 % of the queries are write operations, while range select and table scan operations are not included at all.

The drawbacks of the separation of OLTP and OLAP, the missing support for applications that expose a mixed workload, and the misconception of the nature of OLTP in the first place drove Plattner to design a common database approach for OLTP and OLAP [Pla09, Pla11b, Pla11a]: SanssouciDB provides a common database for OLTP and OLAP and provides adequate performance by leveraging modern hardware technology: mainly the storage of all data in main memory and the utilization of multi-core processors. Although it supports a column- and row-oriented data layout, it puts heavy emphasis on the use of a columnar layout as (i) it is the best match for OLAP workloads, (ii) it has been shown that even OLTP applications have a portion of over 80 % read queries, and (iii) also mixed workloads are dominated by analytical queries.

2.2.3 State-of-the-Art In-Memory Database Management Systems

Summary: This subsection lists state-of-the-art in-memory database management systems.

In this subsection we present a selection of academic and industry in-memory database management systems which are considered state-of-the-art in alphabetical order. We describe their main characteristics, starting with the systems from academia:

- **HyPer (Technical University Munich)** [KNI+11, Neu11] is a main memory database hybrid system that supports row and columnar data layout with the goal of supporting OLTP and OLAP workloads. To guarantee good performance for both workloads simultaneously, HyPer creates snapshots of the transactional data with the help of hardware-assisted replication mechanisms. Data durability is ensured via logging onto a non-volatile storage, high-availability can be achieved by deploying a second hot-standby server. The separate data snapshots for OLTP and OLAP workloads allow conflict-free multi-threaded query processing as well as the deployment to several servers to increase the OLAP throughput [MRR+13].
- **HYRISE (Hasso-Plattner-Institut)** [GKP+10, GCMK+12] is a main memory storage engine that provides dynamic vertical partitioning of the tables it stores. This means that fragments of a single table can either be stored in a row- or column-oriented manner with the intention of supporting OLTP, OLAP, and mixed workloads. HYRISE features a layout algorithm based on a main memory cost model in order to find the best hybrid data layout for a given workload.
- **MonetDB (Centrum Wiskunde and Informatica)** [BGvK+06, BKM08a] is a main memory columnar database management system that is optimized for the bandwidth bottleneck between CPU and main memory. The optimizations include cache-conscious algorithms, data compression, and the modeling of main memory access costs as an input parameter for query optimization. MonetDB is purely intended for executing OLAP workloads and does not support transactions or durability.

The following main memory database systems from industry are presented:

- **IBM solidDB** [MWV+13] is a relational database management system that can either be deployed as an in-memory cache for traditional database systems, such as IBM's DB2 [HS13], or as a stand-alone database. In both cases, it exposes an SQL interface to applications. When deployed as a stand-alone database it offers an in-memory as well as a disk-based storage engine. The in-memory engine uses a trie data structure for indexing, where the nodes in the trie are optimized for modern processor cache sizes. The trie nodes point to data stored consecutively in arrays in main memory. When using the in-memory storage, snapshot-consistent checkpointing [WH1] to disk is used for ensuring durability. IBM is positioning solidDB as a database for application areas such as banking, retail, or telecom [MWV+13].

- **Microsoft SQL Server** has two components which are tailored for in-memory data management: the in-memory database engine Hekaton [DFI$^+$13], which is optimized for OLTP workloads, and xVelocity [Doc13], which is a columnstore index and an analytics engine designed for OLAP workloads. Hekaton stores data either via lock-free hash tables [Mic02] or via lock-free B-trees [LSS13]. In order to improve transactional throughput, Hekaton is able to compile requests to native code. xVelocity offers an in-memory columnar index—not a memory resident columnar storage—that supports data compression and can be utilized by the xVelocity analytics engine, to provide analytical capabilities in conjunction with Microsoft Excel. However, Microsoft SQL Server also offers an updateable columnar storage engine [LCF$^+$13] which stores its data on SSD/disk. Microsoft SQL server is positioned as a general-purpose database.
- **SAP HANA** [FCP$^+$12] is an in-memory database that supports row- and column-oriented storage in a hybrid engine for supporting OLTP, OLAP as well as mixed workloads (see Sect. 2.2.2). In addition, it features a graph and text processing engine for semi- and unstructured data management within the same system. HANA is mainly intended to be used in the context of business applications and can be queried via SQL, SQL Script, MDX, and other domain-specific languages. It supports multiversion concurrency control and ensures durability by logging to SSD. A unique aspect of HANA is its support of transactional workloads via the column store [KGT$^+$10]: the highly compressed column store is accompanied by an additional write-optimized buffer called delta store. The content of the delta is periodically merged into the column store. This architecture provides both fast read and write performance.
- **VoltDB** [SW13] is an in-memory database designed for OLTP workloads and implements the design of the academic H-Store project [KKN$^+$08]. VoltDB persists its data in a row-oriented data layout in main memory and applies check-pointing and transaction logging for providing durability. It boosts transactional throughput by analyzing transactions at compile time, and compiles them as stored procedures which are invoked by the user at run-time with individual parameters. It is designed for a multi-node setup where data is partitioned horizontally and replicated across nodes to provide high availability. VoltDB is relatively young (first release in 2010) and positions itself as a scalable database for transaction processing.

2.3 Parallel Database Management Systems

Summary: This section introduces parallel database management systems which are a variation of distributed database management systems with the intention to execute a query as fast as possible.

As mentioned in Chap. 1, Özsu and Valduriez [ÖV11] define a *distributed database* as

> a collection of multiple, logically interrelated databases distributed over a computer network. A distributed database management system is then defined as the software system that permits the management of the distributed database system and makes the distribution transparent to the users.

The two important terms in these definitions are *logically interrelated* and *distributed over a computer network*. Özsu and Valduriez mention that the typical challenges tackled by distributed database systems include, for example, the aspect of data placement, distributed query processing, distributed concurrency control, and deadlock management, ensuring reliability and availability as well as the integration of heterogeneous databases.

The term *distributed over a computer network* makes no assumption whether the network is a wide area or local area network. A database system that is running on a set of nodes which are connected via a fast network inside a cabinet or inside a data center can be classified as a *parallel database system*. According to Özsu and Valduriez [ÖV11] this can be seen as an revision and extension of a distributed database system. According to DeWitt and Gray [DG92], a parallel database system exploits the parallel nature of an underlying computing system in order to provide high-performance and high-availability.

2.3.1 Shared-Memory Versus Shared-Disk Versus Shared-Nothing

Summary: This subsection introduces and compares different parallel database management system architectures and reflects those in the context of main memory databases.

As briefly summarized in Chap. 1, one fundamental and much debated aspect of a parallel DBMS is its architecture. The architecture influences how the available hardware resources are shared and interconnected. As shown in Fig. 2.9, there

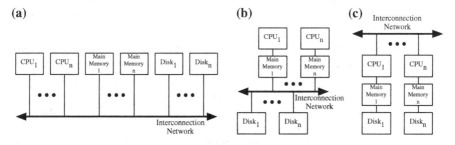

Fig. 2.9 Three different parallel DBMS architectures. **a** Shared-Memory. **b** Shared-Disk. **c** Shared-Nothing

are three different parallel DBMS textbook architectures [ÖV11, DG92, DMS13]: shared-memory, shared-storage (or shared-disk or shared-data), and shared-nothing:

Shared-memory (or shared-everything) (see Fig. 2.9a) is an architectural approach where all processors share direct access to any main memory module and to all disks over an interconnection. Examples for shared-memory DBMS are DBS3 [BCV91] and Volcano [Gra94b]. Shared-memory provides the advantages of an architecturally simple solution: there is no need for complex distributed locking or commit protocols as the lock manager and buffer pool are both stored in the memory system where they can be accessed uniformly by all processors [ERAEB05, DMS13]. In addition, the shared-memory approach is great for parallel processing: inter-query parallelism is an inherent property as all processors share all underlying resources, which means that any query can be executed by any processor. Intra-query parallelism can also be easily achieved due to the shared resources. Shared-memory has two major disadvantages: the extensibility is limited as all the communication between all resources goes over a shared interconnection. For example, a higher number of processors causes conflicts with the shared-memory resource which degrades performance [TS90]. The biggest drawback of shared-memory is its limited availability. Since the memory space is shared by all processors, a memory fault will affect many processors and potentially lead to a corrupted or unavailable database. Although the research community addressed this problem by work on fault-tolerant shared-memory [SMHW02], the shared-memory architecture never had much traction outside academic work and had its peak in the nineties (in terms of available products in industry and published research papers).

Shared-storage (or shared-disk or shared-data) (see Fig. 2.9b) is an architectural approach where processors each have their own memory, but they share access to a single collection of disks. The term shared-disk is a bit confusing in the way that it suggests that rotating disks are an integral part. This is not the case, but hard drive disks were the commonly used storage device when the term was coined. Nowadays a shared-storage architecture can be realized by storing data on disk, SSD, or even keeping it main memory resident (e.g. see Texas Memory Systems RamSan-440 [ME13] or RAMCloud [OAE+11]), typically in the form of a storage area network (SAN) or a network-attached storage (NAS). However, each processor in a shared-storage approach can copy data from the database in its local memory for query processing. Conflicting access can be avoided by global locking or protocols for maintaining data coherence [MN92]. Examples for shared-storage systems are IBM IMS [KLB+12] or Sybase IQ [Moo11]. Shared-storage brings the advantage that it is very extensible as an increase in the overall processing and storage capacity can be done by adding more processors respectively disks. Since each processor has its own memory, interference on the disks can be minimized. The coupling of main memory and processor results in an isolation of a memory module from other processors which results in better availability. As each processor can access all data, load-balancing is trivial (e.g. distributing load in a round-robin manner over all processors). The downsides are an increased coordination effort between the processors in terms of distributed database system protocols, and the shared-disks becoming a bottleneck (similar to the shared-memory approach, sharing a resource over an interconnection is always a potential bottleneck).

Shared-nothing (see Fig. 2.9c) is an architectural approach where each memory and disk is owned by some processor which acts as a server for that data. The Gamma Database Machine Project [DGS+90] or VoltDB [SW13] are examples for shared-nothing architectures. The biggest advantage of a shared-nothing architecture is reducing interferences and resource conflicts by minimizing resource sharing. Operating on the data inside a local machine allows operating with full raw memory and disk performance, high-availability can be achieved by replicating data onto multiple nodes. With careful partitioning across the different machines, a linear speed-up and scale-up can be achieved for simple workloads [ÖV11]. A shared-nothing architecture has also its downsides: the complete decoupling of all resources introduces a higher complexity when implementing distributed database functions (e.g. providing high-availability). Load balancing also becomes more difficult as it is highly dependent on the chosen partition criteria, which makes load balancing based on data location and not actual load of the system. This also impacts the extensibility as adding new machines requires a reevaluation and potentially a reorganization of the existing data partitioning.

When comparing the different architectures one can conclude that there is no better or worse and no clear winner. The different architectures simply offer different trade-offs with various degrees of trading resource sharing against system complexity. Consequently, this is a much debated topic. For example, Rahm [Rah93] says that

> A comparison between shared-disk and shared-nothing reveals many potential benefits for shared-disk with respect to parallel query processing. In particular, shared-disk supports more flexible control over the communication overhead for intratransaction parallelism, and a higher potential for dynamic load balancing and efficient processing of mixed OLTP/query workloads.

DeWitt, Madden, and Stonebraker [DMS13] argue that

> Shared-nothing does not typically have nearly as severe bus or resource contention as shared-memory or shared-disk machines, shared-nothing can be made to scale to hundreds or even thousands of machines. Because of this, it is generally regarded as the best-scaling architecture. Shared-nothing clusters also can be constructed using very low-cost commodity PCs and networking hardware.

Hogan [Hog13] summarizes his take on the discussion with

> The comparison between shared-disk and shared-nothing is analogous to comparing automotive transmissions. Under certain conditions and, in the hands of an expert, the manual transmission provides a modest performance improvement ... Similarly, shared-nothing can be tuned to provide superior performance ... Shared-disk, much like an automatic transmission, is easier to set-up and it adjusts over time to accommodate changing usage patterns.

When reviewing this discussion in the context of parallel main memory databases, there is a clearer picture: most popular systems such as MonetDB, SAP HANA or VoltDB use a shared-nothing architecture and not a shared-storage approach. In the past, there was a big performance gap between accessing main memory inside a machine and in a remote machine. Consequently, a performance advantage that has been achieved by keeping all data in main memory should not vanish by sending much data over a substantially slower network interconnect. As shown in Sect. 2.1.3, the performance gap between local and remote main memory access performance is closing, which paves the way for discussing a shared-storage architecture for a main memory database.

2.3.2 State-of-the-Art Parallel Database Management Systems

Summary: This subsection presents state-of-the-art shared-storage and shared-nothing parallel database management systems.

In this subsection we present a selection of disk-based and main memory-based as well as shared-storage and shared-nothing parallel database management systems and the different variations thereof. Some of the systems were previously introduced, but this subsection focuses on their ability to be deployed on several servers. We start with shared-storage parallel database management systems:

- **IBM DB2 pureScale** [IBM13] is a disk-based shared-storage solution for IBM's row-oriented DB2 [HS13]. It allows the creation of a parallel DBMS consisting of up to 128 nodes where each node is an instance of DB2 and all nodes share access to a storage system that is based on IBM's General Parallel File System (GPFS) [SH02]. Each database node utilizes local storage for caching or maintaining a bufferpool. In addition to the local bufferpools per node, there is also a global bufferpool that keeps record of all pages that have been updated, inserted or deleted. This global bufferpool is used in conjunction with a global lock manager: before any node can make for example an update, it has to request the global lock. After data modification, the global lock manager invalidates all local copies of the respective page in the local memory of the nodes. PureScale offers so called cluster services which, for example, orchestrate the recovery process in the event of a downtime. GPFS stores the data in blocks of a configured size and also supports striping and mirroring to ensure high-availability and improved performance.
- **MySQL on MEMSCALE** [MSFD11a,b] is shared-storage deployment of MySQL on MEMSCALE, which is a hardware-based shared-memory system that claims to scale gracefully by not sharing cores nor caches, and therefore working without a coherency protocol. This approach uses the main memory storage engine of MySQL (known as heap or memory) and replaces the common *malloc* by a library function that allocates memory from the MEMSCALE shared-memory. As a consequence, all properties of MySQL are still present so that queries can be executed in a multithreaded, ACID compliant manner with row-level locking.
- **MySQL on RamSan** [ME13] is a shared-storage solution where MySQL utilizes the storage space provided by a storage area network that keeps all data resident in main memory called RamSan. RamSan was originally developed by Texas Memory Systems (now acquired by IBM). It acts as a traditional storage area network, but depending on the configuration keeps all data in main memory

modules such as DDR, and uses additional SSDs for non-volatile storage. RamSan provides the advantage that it is transparent to a database system, such as MySQL, that main memory-based storage is being used, but incorporates the downside that data access is not optimized for main memory.

- **ScaleDB** [Sca13] implements a shared-storage architecture that consists of three different entities, namely database nodes, storage nodes, and a cluster manager. Each database node runs an instance of MySQL server that is equipped with a custom ScaleDB storage engine by utilizing the MySQL feature of pluggable storage engines [MyS13a]. That results in a multithreaded, disk-based, ACID compliant engine that supports row-level locking and operates in read committed mode. All database nodes share common access to the data inside the storage nodes. ScaledDB manages the data in block-structured files with each individual file being broken into blocks of a fixed size. These blocks are stored twice for providing high-availability and are distributed randomly across the storage nodes. In addition, ScaleDB also features a cluster manager that is a distributed lock manager that synchronizes lock requests of different nodes.
- **Sybase IQ** [Syb13a] is a shared-storage, columnar, relational database system that is mainly used for data analytics. As depicted in the Sybase IQ 15 sizing guide [Syb13b], a set of database nodes accesses a commonly shared storage that holds all data. Among the database nodes is a primary server (or coordinator node) that manages all global read-write transactions and maintains the global catalog and metadata. In order to maximize the throughput when operating on the shared storage system, Sybase IQ strips data with the intention of utilizing as many disks in parallel as possible.

The following shared-nothing parallel database management systems are presented:

- **C-Store** [SAB⁺05] and its commercial counterpart **Vertica** [LFV⁺12] are disk-based columnar parallel DBMSs based on a shared-nothing architecture. The data distribution in Vertica is done by splitting tuples among nodes by a hash-based ring style segmentation scheme. Within each node, tuples are physically grouped into local segments which are used as a unit of transfer when nodes are being added to or removed from the cluster in order to speed up the data transfer. Vertica allows defining how often a data item is being replicated across the cluster (called k-saftey), realizing thereby high-availability, and allows the operator of the cluster to set the desired tradeoff between hardware costs and availability guarantees.
- **MySQL Cluster** [DF06] enables MySQL (MySQL [MyS13b] is one of the most popular open-source relational DBMS) to be used as a shared-nothing parallel DBMS. MySQL Cluster partitions data across all nodes in the system by hash-based partitioning according to the primary key of a table. The database administrator can choose a different partitioning schema by specifying another key of a table as partitioning criteria. In addition, data is synchronously replicated to multiple nodes for guaranteeing availability. Durability is ensured in a way that each node writes logs to disk in addition to checkpointing the data regularly. In a MySQL cluster, there are three different type of nodes: a management node that is

used for configuration and monitoring of the cluster, a data node which stores parts
of the tables, and a SQL node that accepts queries from clients and automatically
communicates with all other nodes that hold a piece of the data needed to execute
a query.

- **Postgres eXtensible Cluster** (Postgres-XC) [Pos13, BS13] is a solution to deploy
  PostgreSQL as a disk-based, row oriented, shared-nothing parallel DBMS. A
  Postgres-XC cluster consists of three different types of entities: a global transaction manager, a coordinator, and datanodes. The global transaction manager is
  a central instance in a Postgres-XC cluster and enables multi-version concurrency
  control (e.g. by issuing unique transaction IDs). The coordinator accepts queries
  from an application and coordinates their execution by requesting a transaction ID
  from the global transaction manager, determining which datanodes are needed for
  answering a query and sending them the respective part of the query. The overall
  data is partitioned across datanodes where each datanode executes (partial) queries
  on its own data. Data can also be replicated across the datanodes in order to provide
  high-availability.

- **SAP HANA** [FML$^+$12] is an in-memory parallel DBMS based on a shared-nothing
  architecture [LKF$^+$13]. A database table in HANA can be split by applying round-
  robin, hash- or range-based partitioning strategies: the database administrator can
  assign the resulting individual partitions to individual HANA nodes either directly
  or based on the suggestions of automated partitioning tools. There are two different
  types of nodes: a coordinator node and a worker node. A database query issued
  by a client gets send to a coordinator node first. A coordinator is responsible for
  compiling a distributed query plan based on data locality or issuing global transaction tokens. The query plan then gets executed by a set of worker nodes where
  each worker node operates on its local data. HANA also features a distributed
  cost-based query optimizer that lays out the execution of single database operators which span multiple worker nodes. High-availability is ensured by hardware
  redundancy which allows to provide a stand-by server for a worker node that takes
  over immediately if the associated node fails [SAP13]. Durability is ensured by
  persisting transaction logs, savepoints, and snapshots to SSD or disk in order to
  recover from host failures or to support the restart of the complete system.

- **MonetDB** [BGvK$^+$06] is an in-memory columnar DBMS that can be deployed as a
  shared-nothing cluster. MonetDB is a research project, it comes with the necessary
  primitives such as networking support and setting up a cluster by connecting
  individual nodes each running MonetDB. This foundation can be used to add
  shared-nothing data partitioning features and distributed query optimizations for
  running data analytics [MC13]. MonetDB is also used as a platform for researching
  novel distributed data processing schemes: for example the Data Cyclotron [GK10]
  project creates a virtual network ring based on RDMA-enabled network facilities
  where data is perpetually being passed through the ring, and individual nodes pick
  up data fragments for query processing.

- **Teradata Warehouse** [Ter13, CC11] is a shared-nothing parallel database system used for data analytics. The architecture consists of three major component
  types: a parsing engine, an access module processor (AMP), and the BYNET

framework. The parsing engine accepts queries from the user, creates query plans and distributes them over the network (BYNET framework) to the corresponding access module processors. An AMP is a separate physical machine that runs an instance of the Teradata Warehouse database management system which solely operates on the disks of that machine. The disks inside an AMP are organized in redundant arrays to prevent data loss. The data is partitioned across all AMPs by a hash partitioning schema in order to distribute the data evenly and reduce the risk of bottlenecks. Teradata warehouse allows configuring dedicated AMPs for hot standby which can seamlessly take over in the case of a failure of an active AMP.

- **VoltDB** [SW13] is a row-oriented in-memory database that can be deployed as a shared-nothing parallel database system. In such a cluster, each server runs an instance of the VoltDB database management system. Tables are partitioned across nodes by hashing the primary key values. In addition, tables can also be replicated across nodes for performance and high-availability. For ensuring high-availability, three mechanisms are in place: k-safety which allows to specify the number k of data replicas in the cluster. Network fault detection evaluates in the case of a network fault which side of the cluster should continue operation based on the completeness of the data. Live node rejoin allows nodes when they restart after a failure to be reintroduced to the running cluster and retrieve their copy of the data. Durability is ensured via snapshots to disks in intervals and command logging.

2.3.3 Database-Aware Storage Systems

Summary: This subsection introduces database-aware storage systems which are storage systems that support the execution of database operations in order to reduce network communication.

The previous discussion of shared-storage versus shared-nothing architectures describes that each architecture has its advantages: one advantage of a shared-nothing architecture is that a processor performs data operations on the data that is inside the same machine without the need for transferring the data over a network first. Database-aware storage systems [RGF98, Kee99, SBADAD05] aim at bringing that advantage to shared-storage systems by executing database operators directly in the storage system. This approach is based on the idea of active storage/active disks/intelligent disks [AUS98, KPH98] where the computational power inside the storage device is being used for moving computation closer to the data.

The American National Standards Institute (ANSI) Object-based Storage Device (OSD) T10 standard describes a command set for the Small Computer System Interface (SCSI) [sta04] that allows communication between the application and the storage system. This, in turn, is the foundation for the work of Raghuveer, Schlosser, and Iren [RSI07] who use this OSD interface for improving data access for a database application by making the storage device aware of relations, in contrast to just returning blocks of data. However, they do not support the execution of application/database code inside the storage device. This is done in the Diamond project

[HSW$^+$04], as it applies the concept of *early discard* in an active storage system. *Early discard* describes the rejection of to be filtered out data as early as possible. Diamond supports the processing of such filters inside an active disk and makes sure that not requested data is discarded before it reaches the application, such as a database system. Riedel, Gibson, and, Faloutsos [RGF98] evaluate the usage of active disks for a different set of application scenarios including nearest neighbor search in a database and data mining of frequent sets. They conclude that the processing power of a disk drive will always be inferior to server CPUs, but that a storage system usually consists of a lot of disks resulting in the advantage of parallelism, and that combining their computational power with the processors inside the server results in a higher total processing capacity. In addition, the benefit of filtering in the disk reduces the load on the interconnect and brought significant performance advantages for their application scenarios.

An example for a current system that exploits the possibilities of database-aware storage systems is Oracle's Exadata which combines a database and a storage system inside a single appliance: the Exadata storage system supports *Smart-Scan* and Offloading [SBADAD05]. *Smart-Scan* describes the possibility to execute column projections, predicate filtering, and index creation inside the storage system. Offloading enables the execution of more advanced database functions inside the storage system, such as simple joins or the execution of mathematical or analytical functions.

2.3.4 Operator Placement for Distributed Query Processing

Summary: This subsection describes and discusses query, hybrid, and data shipping which are three different approaches how the resources from client and server can be utilized for processing a query in a distributed database management system.

When using a database-aware storage system, the resources from the storage system, as well as the resources from the DBMS, can be utilized for query processing. In the field of distributed query processing, this problem is classified as the exploitation of client resources in the context of client-server database systems. As this problem is originated in a setting where the client is an application and the DBMS acts as a server, the remainder of this section presents a detailed description of the problem including the related work and discusses it in conjunction with database-aware storage systems, where the DBMS is the client and the server is a storage system.

Tanenbaum explains the client-server model by stating that "a client process sends a request to a server process which then does the work and sends back the answer" [Tan07]. Based on that definition, Kossmann gives in his seminal paper *The State of the Art in Distributed Query Processing* [Kos00] (which is in form and content the blueprint for the remainder of this subsection) a description of the client resource exploitation problem:

> The essence of client-server computing is that the database is persistently stored by server machines and that queries are initiated at client machines. The question is whether to execute a query at the client machine at which the query was initiated or at the server machines that

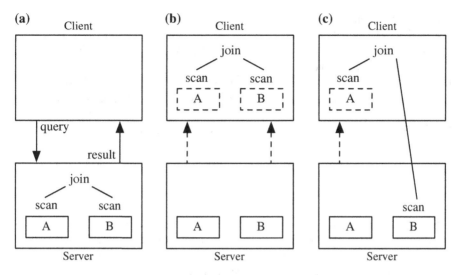

Fig. 2.10 Illustration of query, data, and hybrid shipping (Figure taken from [Kos00]). **a** Query Shipping. **b** Data Shipping. **c** Hybrid Shipping

store the relevant data. In other words, the question is whether to move the query to the data (execution at servers) or to move the data to the query (execution at clients).

This results in the following three approaches:

Query shipping (see Fig. 2.10a) is an approach where the client sends the query in its entirety to the server, the server processes the query and sends back the result. This is the approach that is typical for example for relational DBMSs such as Microsoft SQL Server or IBM DB2.

Data shipping (or data pull) (see Fig. 2.10b) is the opposite solution where the client consumes all the needed data from the server and then processes the query locally. This results in an execution of the query where it originated. Object-oriented databases often work after the data shipping principle as the client consumes the objects as a whole and then does the processing.

Hybrid shipping (see Fig. 2.10c) is a combination of the two previous approaches. As shown by Franklin, Jónsson, and Kossmann [FJK96], hybrid shipping allows executing some query operators at the server side, but also pulling data to and processing it at the client side. As shown in Fig. 2.10c, data region A is being pulled and scanned at the client's side. Data region B is scanned at the server's side, and the results are then transferred to the client where they are joined with the results from the scan on data region A.

The three different approaches imply a number of design decisions when creating a model that supports the decision where the execution of each individual database operator that belongs to a query is being placed. Those decisions are: (a) the site selection itself which determines where each individual operator is being executed, (b) where to decide the site selection, (c) what parameters should be considered when doing the site selection, and (d) when to determine the site selection.

Table 2.2 Site selection for different classes of database operators for query, data, and hybrid shipping (Figure taken from [Kos00])

Database operator	Query shipping	Data shipping	Hybrid shipping
Display	Client	Client	Client
Update	Server	Client	Client or server
Binary operators (e.g. join)	Producer of left or right input	Consumer (i.e. client)	Consumer or producer of left or right input
Unary operators (e.g. sort, group-by)	Producer	Consumer (i.e. client)	Consumer or producer
Scan	server	Client	Client or server

Site selection in conjunction with the client resource exploitation problem says that each individual database operator has a site annotation that indicates where this operator is going to be executed [Kos00]. As shown in Table 2.2, different annotations are possible per operator class: display operations return the result of a query which always has to happen at the client. All other operators in a data shipping approach are executed at the client site as well or in other words at the site where the data is consumed. Query shipping executes all operators at the server site or where the data is produced (e.g. by the execution of a previous operator). Hybrid shipping supports both annotations. The question **where** to make the site selection depends on several factors, most notably the number of servers in the system: if there is only one server, it makes sense to let the server decide the site selection as it knows its own current load [HF86]. If there are many servers, there might be no or only little information gained by executing it at the server site as a single server has no complete knowledge of the system. In addition, the site selection itself is also an operation that consumes resources which can be scaled with the number of clients if executed at the client. **What** information is considered for the site selection depends on the nature of the site selection algorithm. For example, for a cost-based approach one might want to consider information about the database operation itself, such as the amount of data to be traversed or the selectivity, the hardware properties of the client, the server, as well as the interconnect or information about the current load of the client and/or the server. If the site selection algorithm is a heuristic, simple information such as the class of the current database operation and the selectivity might be sufficient (e.g. executing a scan operator at the server site if the selectivity is greater than x). Three different approaches are possible with regards to deciding **when** site selection occurs: a static, a dynamic, and a two-step optimization approach. A static approach can be chosen if the queries are known and compiled at the same time when the application itself is being compiled. This allows also to decide on the site selection at compile time. Only in exceptional situations, such as a change in the predetermined queries, doesa reevaluation of the site selection occur [CAK$^+$81]. This approach works well if queries and workload are static, but performs poorly with a fluctuating or changing workload. A simple dynamic approach generates alternative site selection plans at design time and chooses the site selection plan during query execution that for example best matches the assumptions about the current load of the system. If that repeatedly results in poor performance, a new set of site selection plans can be generated [CG94]. This can be especially useful if certain servers are not responsive [UFA98] or if the initial assumptions of e.g. the sizes of intermediate results turned out to be wrong [KD98]. Two-step optimization is a more advanced dynamic approach that determines the site selection just before the query execution. This is achieved by a decomposition of the overall query execution into two steps [Kos00]. First, a query plan is generated that specifies the join order, join methods, and access paths. This first step has the same complexity as the query plan creation in a centralized system. Second, right before executing the query plan, it is determined where every operator is being executed. As the second step only carries out the site selection for a single query at a time, its complexity is reasonably low and can also be done during query execution. As a consequence, it is assumed that this approach reduces the overall complexity of distributed query optimization and is hereby popular for distributed and parallel database systems [HM95, GGS96]. The advantages of the two-step optimization are the aforementioned low complexity and the ability to consider the current state of the system at the time of query execution which can be used for workload distribution [CL86] and to exploit caching [FJK96]. The downside of decoupling query plan creation and site selection is ignoring the placement of data across servers during query plan creation as it might result in a site selection plan with unnecessary high communication costs [Kos00].

The previous explanations are a general take on the client resource exploitation and the resulting site selection problem. They include the underlying assumption that every operator in a query can be executed at the client or the server. However, this might not be the case as not all database operators are available at both sites. This limits the site selection scope to a subset or a set of classes of database operators depending on which are available at both sites. In addition, the execution order of the operators according to the query plan also limits the site selection (e.g. a query plan foresees that two relations are scanned and the results of the scan operations are joined). The scan operators are available at the client and server sites, the join operator is only available at the server. In this case, executing the scans at the client site results in an unreasonably high communication overhead as both relations have to be shipped in their entirety to the client and then the scan results have to be shipped back to the server for processing the join. The availability of operators at a site depends on which kind of system acts as the client and the server. If the client is an application and the server is a relational database management system, then the entirety of database operators is available at the server site. The default mode is to ship the query to the DBMS and retrieve the result. It is possible that some operators are also available at the client site (e.g. a scan and a group-by operator). That allows hybrid shipping for queries that facilitate both, and makes data shipping an option for queries that only consists of these two types of operators. In such a setting, all possible queries can be executed with query shipping, a subset of them with hybrid shipping and an even smaller subset with data shipping (as depicted in Fig. 2.11). The situation is reversed when the client is a relational DBMS and the server is a database-aware storage system. If the database-aware storage system has a scan

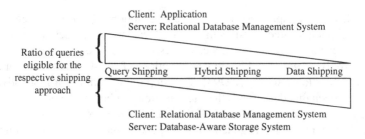

Fig. 2.11 Depicting the ratio of queries which are eligible for query, hybrid or data shipping in correspondence with a relational DBMS either acting as server or client

operator implemented, all queries can be executed with data shipping, queries which involve a scan can be executed via hybrid shipping and queries solely consisting of scans have the option of using a query shipping approach.

2.4 Cloud Storage Systems

Summary: This section introduces and classifies cloud storage systems and describes how they differ from traditional database and file systems.

The paradigm of cloud computing describes the provisioning of information technology infrastructure, services, and applications over the Internet. Typical characteristics are the on-demand availability of such resources, their quick adaption to changing workloads, and the billing based on actual usage. From a data management perspective, two different types of cloud storage systems have been created to manage and persist large amounts of data created and consumed by cloud computing applications: (a) So called NoSQL[2] systems include distributed key-value stores, such as Amazon Dynamo [DHJ+07] or Project Voldemort, wide column stores such as Google Bigtable [CDG+06] or Cassandra [LM10] as well as document and graph stores. (b) Distributed file systems such as Google File System (GFS) [GGL03] or Hadoop Distributed File System (HDFS) [SKRC10]. The remainder of this section explains the motivation for building these cloud storage systems, and their underlying concepts, as well as how they differ from traditional database and file systems.

The previous section explains that parallel database management systems combine the resources of multiple computers to accelerate the execution of queries as well as increase the overall data processing capacity. Such systems were greatly challenged with the advent of e-commerce and Internet-based services offered by companies

---

[2]There is no explicit explanation what the abbreviation NoSQL stands for, but it is most commonly agreed that it means "not only SQL". This term does not reject the query language SQL, but rather expresses that the design of relational database management systems is unsuitable for large-scale cloud applications [Bur10] (see Eric Brewer's CAP theorem [Bre00, Bre12] as explained later in this Section).

such as Amazon, eBay or Google in the mid-nineties. These companies not only grew rapidly in their overall size, they also did it in a comparatively short period of time with unpredictable growth bursts. This development put big emphasis on the aspects of *scalability* and *elasticity* in the context of data storage and processing systems. Scalability is defined as

> a desirable property of a system, which indicates its ability to either handle growing amounts of work in a graceful manner or its ability to improve throughput when additional resources (typically hardware) are added. A system whose performance improves after adding hardware, proportionally to the capacity added, is said to be a scalable system [AEADE11].

Elasticity hardens the scalability property as it focuses on the quality of the workload adaption process—e.g. when resources have been added—in terms such as money or time. Elasticity can be defined as

> the ability to deal with load variations by adding more resources during high load or consolidating the tenants to fewer nodes when the load decreases, all in a live system without service disruption, is therefore critical for these systems. ... Elasticity is critical to minimize operating costs while ensuring good performance during high loads. It allows consolidation of the system to consume less resources and thus minimize the operating cost during periods of low load while allowing it to dynamically scale up its size as the load decreases [AEADE11].[3]

For example, the Internet-based retailer Amazon initially used off-the-shelf relational database management systems as the data processing backend for their Internet platform. The Amazon Chief Technology Officer Werner Vogels explains [Vog07] that Amazon had to perform short-cycled hardware upgrades to their database machines in their early days. Each upgrade would only provide sufficient data processing performance for a couple of months until the next upgrade was due to the company's extreme growth. This was followed by attempts to tune their relational database systems by simplifying the database schema, introducing various caching layers or partitioning the data differently. At some point the engineering team at Amazon decided to evaluate the data processing needs at Amazon and create their own data processing infrastructure accordingly. These data processing needs reveal [Vog07] that at Amazon e.g. about 65 % of the data access is based on the primary key only, about 15 % of the data access exposes lot of writes in combination with the need for strong consistency, and 99.9 % of the data access has a need for low latency where a response time of less than 15 ms is expected. The variety in their data processing needs is covered by a set of solutions where the most prominent one is Amazon Dynamo.

Amazon Dynamo [DHJ+07] is a distributed key-value store. Since the majority of data operations at Amazon encompass primary key access only and require low latency, Dynamo is designed for storing and retrieving key-value pairs (also referred to as objects). Dynamo implements a distributed hash table where the different nodes that hold data of that hash table are organized as a ring. The data distribution is done

---

[3]The definitions and usage of the terms scalability and elasticity are much discussed in the computer science community as they are not strictly quantifiable [Hil90].

via consistent hashing. However, a hash-based data partitioning onto physical nodes would lead to a non-uniform data and load distribution due to the random position assignment of each node in the ring and the basic algorithm is oblivious to the heterogeneity in the performance of nodes. This is addressed by the introduction of virtual nodes (which can be thought of as namespaces), where a single virtual node is being mapped onto different physical nodes: this allows for providing high-availability and elasticity by changing the number of physical nodes assigned to a virtual node upon workload changes. As a result, nodes can be added and removed from Dynamo without any need for manual partitioning and redistribution. Consistency is facilitated by object versioning [Lam78]. The consistency among replicas during updates is maintained by a quorum-like technique and a decentralized replica synchronization protocol. These features in combination make Dynamo a scalable, highly-available, completely decentralized system with minimal need for manual administration. Amazon Dynamo is just one example of a distributed key-value store, but it is conceptually similar to other popular distributed key-value stores such as Riak [Klo10] or Project Voldemort [SKG$^+$12]. Google Bigtable [CDG$^+$06] and Cassandra [LM10] are examples for wide column stores (also known as extensible record stores [Cat11]): for example Google Bigtable implements a sparse, distributed, persistent multi-dimensional map indexed by a row key, a column key, and some kind of versioning information such as a timestamp or versioning number. This multi-dimensional map is partitioned in a cluster in the following way: the rows of a map are split across nodes with the assignment being done by ranges and based on hashing. Each column of a map is described as a column family, the contained data is of the same type and its data is being distributed over multiple nodes. Such a column family must not be mistaken for a relational database column that implies that related data is physically collocated, but can be seen more as a namespace. The motivation for using such wide column stores over simple distributed key-value stores is the more expressive data model, that provides a simple approach to model references between data items [CDG$^+$06].

How a cloud storage system such as Amazon Dynamo differs from a relational DBMS and how it addresses the previously mentioned scalability shortcomings can be illustrated with the Consistency, Availability, and Partition Tolerance (CAP) theorem by Eric Brewer [Bre00, Bre12]. In this theorem

> consistency means that all nodes see the same data at the same time, availability is a guarantee that every request receives a response about whether it was successful or failed and partition tolerance lets the system continue to operate despite arbitrary message loss.

The theorem states that a distributed system can provide two properties at the same time, but not three. Relational DBMSs provide consistency and availability, cloud storage systems provide availability and partition tolerance. This is done by relaxing the ACID constraints in cloud storage systems as it significantly reduces the communication overhead in a distributed system, providing simple data access APIs instead of complex query interfaces, and schema-free data storage [Bur10].

Another category of cloud storage systems are distributed filesystems. Distributed filesystems in general have been available for over 30 years, their purpose is to "allow users of physically distributed computers to share data and storage resources by using a common file system" [LS90]. Well-cited examples are Sun's Network File System (NFS) [SGK+88] and the Sprite Network File System [OCD+88]. However, a distributed file system—such as the Google File System—which is designed to act as a cloud storage system, differs from traditional distributed filesystems in a similar way as a distributed key-value storage differs from a relational database management system. It weakens consistency, reduces synchronization operations along with the introduction of replicating data multiple times in order to scale gracefully and provide high-availability. This can be illustrated by reviewing the underlying assumptions and requirements that led to the design of the Google File System [GGL03]: the file system is built from many inexpensive commodity components where hardware failures are the norm not the exception, which means that fault-tolerance and auto-recovery need to be built into the system. Files can be huge, bandwidth is more important than latency, reads are mostly sequential and writes are dominated by append operations. The corresponding Google File System architecture foresees that a GFS cluster has a single master server, multiple chunkservers and they are accessed by multiple clients. Files in GFS are divided into fixed-size chunks, where each chunk is identified by a unique 64-bit chunk handle, the size of a chunk is 64 MB, and chunks are replicated at least three times throughout the cluster. A master server maintains all file system metadata such as namespaces, access control information, the mappings from files to chunks as well as the locations from the different chunks on the chunkservers. Each chunkserver stores its chunks as separate files in a Linux file system. If a client wants to access a file, it contacts the master server which provides it with the chunk server locations as well as the file-to-chunk mappings: the client is then enabled to autonomously contact the chunkservers. This allows clients to read, write, and append records in parallel at the price of a relaxed consistency model (e.g. it may take some time until updates are perpetuated to all replicas): these relaxed consistency guarantees have to be covered by the applications that run on top of GFS (e.g. by application-level checkpointing).

With the increasing popularity of cloud storage systems emerged the need to execute more complex operations on the stored data than simple data retrieval and modification operations. This need is addressed by Google's MapReduce programming model [DG08] that was built for being used in conjunction with Google Bigtable or the Google File System. The idea of MapReduce is to process large sets of key-value pairs with a parallel, distributed algorithm on a cluster: the algorithm performs at first a Map() operation that performs filter operations on key-value pairs and creates corresponding intermediate results followed by a Reduce() operation which groups the intermediate results foe example by combining all results that share the same key. The simplicity of this approach, the ability to quickly identify non-interleaving data partitions, and the ability to execute the respective sub-operations independently, enable a great degree of parallelism.

2.4.1 State-of-the-Art Cloud Storage Systems

Summary: This subsection presents state-of-the-art cloud storage systems.

   After describing Amazon Dynamo, Google Bigtable, and the Google File System in the previous subsection, we discuss additional state-of-the-art cloud storage systems.

- **Amazon Dynamo** [DHJ$^+$07] see previous Sect. 2.4.
- **Google Bigtable** [CDG$^+$06] see previous Sect. 2.4.
- **Google File System** [GGL03] see previous Sect. 2.4.
- **Hadoop** [Whi09] and the **Hadoop Distributed File System** (HDFS) [SKRC10] are open-source implementations based on the concepts of Google's MapReduce and the Google File System. HDFS has a similar architecture as GFS as it deploys a central entity called namenode that maintains all the meta information about the HDFS cluster. So called datanodes hold the data which gets replicated across racks, and clients that directly interact with datanodes after retrieving the needed metadata from the namenode. HDFS differs from GFS in the details (e.g. HDFS uses 128 MB blocks instead of GFS's 64 MB chunks). In HDFS a client can freely choose against which datanode it wants to write, and HDFS is aware of the concept of a datacenter rack when it comes to data balancing. Hadoop itself is a framework for executing MapReduce, it includes and utilizes HDFS for storing data, and provides additional modules such as the MapReduce engine: this engine takes care of scheduling and executing MapReduce jobs, and consists of a JobTracker which accepts and dispatches MapReduce jobs from clients and several TaskTrackers which aim to execute the individual jobs as close to the data as possible.
- **Memcached** [Fit04] is a distributed key-value store which is commonly used for caching data in the context of large web applications (e.g. Facebook [NFG$^+$13]). As a consequence, each server in a Memcached cluster keeps its data resident in main memory for performance improvements. Upon a power or hardware failure, the main memory resident data is lost. However, this is not considered harmful as it is cached data, which might be invalidated after potential server recovery. Memcached itself has no support for data recovery, it is expected to be provided by the application (e.g. Memcached is extensively being used at Facebook and the Facebook engineering implemented their own data replication mechanism [NFG$^+$13]). The data in a Memcached cluster is partitioned across servers based on hash values of the to be stored keys: their ranges are mapped to buckets and each server is assigned one or more buckets.
- **Project Voldemort** [SKG$^+$12] is a distributed key-value store developed by the social network LinkedIn and is conceptionally similar to Amazon's Dynamo. Project Voldemort also applies consistent hashing to partition its data across nodes and to replicate data over multiple times with a configurable replication factor. Project Voldemort also does not provide strong consistency, but facilitates a versioning system to ensure that data replicas become consistent at some point.
- **Stanford's RAMCloud** [OAE$^+$11] is a research project that combines the in-memory performance of a solution such as Memcached with the durable,

high-available, and gracefully scaling storage of data as realized by a project such as Bigtable. It does so by keeping all data entirely in DRAM by aggregating the main memory of multiple of commodity servers at scale. In addition, all of these servers are connected via a high-end network such as InfiniBand (as discussed in Sect. 2.1.3) which provides low latency [ROS+11] and a high bandwidth. RAM-Cloud employs randomized techniques to manage the system in a scalable and decentralized fashion and is based on a key-value data model. RAMCloud scatters backup data across hundreds or thousands of disks or SSDs, and harnesses hundreds of servers in parallel to reconstruct lost data. The system uses a log-structured approach for all its data, in DRAM as well as on disk/SSD, which provides high performance both during normal operation and during recovery [ORS+11]. The inner workings are explained in detail in Sect. 3.3.

2.4.2 Combining Database Management and Cloud Storage Systems

Summary: This subsection discusses different approaches of combining database management and cloud storage systems, including the adaptation of each other's features, providing connectors, translating SQL to MapReduce programs, providing specialized SQL engines on top of cloud storage systems, having a hybrid SQL/MapReduce execution, and utilizing a cloud storage system as shared-storage for a DBMS.

The advent of cloud storage systems piqued interest in the DBMS as well as in the cloud storage systems community to evaluate the use and adaptation of each other's features. Initially, this was an unstructured undertaking which for example resulted in the statement by Michael Carey that "it is the wild west out there again" [ACC+10]. Dean Jacobs said "I recently reviewed a large number of 'cloud database' papers for various conferences. Most of these papers were either adding features to distributed key-value stores to make them more usable or removing features from conventional relational databases to make them more scalable" [Jac13]. However, the adaptation of relational query processing features in a cloud storage system eventually became a well-established area of work in academia as demonstrated by the Stratosphere project [Mem13b], which extends the MapReduce model with operators [BEH+10] which are common in relational DBMS.

The advantages and growing popularity of cloud storage systems led to the desire to execute SQL statements against data that is inside a cloud storage system. The different approaches can be put into the following four categories:

- **DBMS to cloud storage system connectors** allow the bidirectional exchange of data between the two systems. Such an approach is commonly used for running ad-hoc queries on the outcome of a MapReduce job by preparing the unstructured data in the cloud storage system and then convert it to structured data inside the DBMS. Those connectors are popular with traditional DBMS vendors as they allow them to label their products as "Hadoop compatible". Examples for such connectors are the Microsoft SQL Server Connector for Apache Hadoop [Cor13] and the HP Vertica Hadoop Distributed File System Connector [Ver13]. The disadvantages of such connectors are that they (a) require an ETL process which forbids ad-hoc querying, (b) transfer the complete to be queried dataset over the network, and (c) create a redundant copy of the dataset.

- **SQL translated to MapReduce** allows sending an SQL query to a cloud storage system such as Hadoop. The SQL query is translated to a set of MapReduce jobs which are then executed by the cluster. This bears the advantages that it (a) utilizes the properties of the cloud storage system in terms of high-availability as well as scalability and (b) integrates into the existing scheduling of MapReduce jobs (as opposed to the previous approach where the extraction of data creates an unexpected extra load). The main disadvantages are that (a) the accepted SQL is a SQL dialect and not SQL-standard conform and (b) the translation overhead and the MapReduce batch-oriented execution style prevent ad-hoc queries. Facebook's Hive [TSJ+09] is an example of a system that uses such an approach.
- **Specialized SQL engines on top of cloud storage systems** accept SQL-like queries. They execute the queries not by translating them to MapReduce jobs, but by shipping custom database operators to the data nodes. Systems that fall into that category are the row-oriented Google F1 [SOE+12] and the column-oriented Google Dremel [MGL+10]. For example Google Dremel operates on GFS and exploits the GFS interfaces that allows code execution on chunkservers and thereby to ship and execute operators. This results in the advantage of being able to execute ad-hoc queries as well as collocating data and their processing. The big disadvantages of such an approach are that (a) such specialized SQL engines are not SQL-standard compliant and (b) they only provide poor coverage of the common SQL operators. These disadvantages eliminate the use of existing tools and the ability to execute applications which expose SQL-standard compliant queries.
- **Hybrid SQL and MapReduce execution** aims at combining both of the previous approaches: an SQL query submitted to the system gets analyzed and then parts of it are processed via MapReduce and other parts with the execution of native database operators. That allows to determine the mix of MapReduce and database operator execution based on the type of query: for executing ad-hoc queries MapReduce-style execution is avoided as much as possible whereas it is preferred for queries at massive scale in combination with the need for fault tolerance. Examples for such systems are HadoopDB [BPASP11] or Polybase [DHN+13].

Another category of research that focuses on the combination of database management and cloud storage systems is the **use of cloud storage systems as shared-storage for parallel DBMS**. Whereas the previously explained approaches trim the SQL coverage and sacrifice the compliance with the SQL standard, this approach takes a standard relational query processor or DBMS and utilizes the cloud storage system instead of a classic shared-disk storage.

- **Building a Database on S3** [BFG$^+$08] by Brantner et al. demonstrates the use of Amazon S3 as a shared-disk for persisting the data from a MySQL database. This work maps the elements from the MySQL B-tree to key-value objects and provides a corresponding custom MySQL storage engine that allows for prototypical experiments. It also introduces a set of protocols which show how different levels of consistency can be implemented using S3. Driven by the TPC-W benchmark, the trade-offs between performance, response time, and costs (in terms of US dollars) are discussed.
- **Running a transactional Database on top of RAMCloud** [Pil12] by Pilman takes a similar conceptual approach, but utilizes RAMCloud instead of Amazon S3. The motivation for using RAMCloud is to exploit its performance advantages provided by in-memory data storage and RDMA capabilities. The work by Pilman presents two different architectures: one where a MySQL instance runs exclusively on a RAMCloud cluster, and the other one where several instances of MySQL run on a RAMCloud cluster. A benchmark is presented that executes TPC-W and uses MySQL with InnoDB as a baseline. The experiments show that "we can run MySQL on top of a key-value store without any loss of performance or scalability but still gain the advantages this architecture provides. We have the desired elasticity and several applications could run in the same network using each its own database system, but all on the same key-value store" [Pil12].

2.5 Classification

Summary: This section classifies related work as presented throughout the chapter.

After an extensive explanation of the background and the related work in the previous sections of this chapter, this section presents a compact overview on the related work and the corresponding classification.

This work is positioned in the field of evaluating a parallel DBMS architecture and its implications on query processing. As explained in Sect. 2.3.1, the shared-nothing versus shared storage architecture trade-offs are much discussed in the context of classic storage architectures (e.g. SAN/NAS storage) and a great variety of products from big vendors are available in both markets. It is noteworthy that for main memory resident parallel DBMSs a shared-nothing architecture is dominating: this is due to the intention of not sacrificing the performance advantage of keeping data in main memory, but constantly shipping it over a significantly slower network. However, with the advent of fast switch fabric communication links—as discussed in Sect. 2.1.3—the performance gap between accessing local and remote main memory narrows down and the implications of this development on the architecture discussion for main memory parallel DBMS are not clear yet.

Deploying a parallel DBMS on a cloud storage system is a relatively new area of research. As explained in Sect. 2.4.2, the cloud community has worked out several approaches how to execute SQL-like statements against data in a cloud storage system. Specialized SQL engines on top of cloud storage systems most closely resemble a traditional DBMS as they just use database operators for query execution and neglect the batch-oriented MapReduce paradigm altogether. But even those systems are not SQL-standard compliant and provide their own SQL dialect which makes them uninteresting for the broad range of applications that expose SQL-standard compliant queries. This downside is not inherent to the work from the DBMS community which takes the opposite approach by deploying a standard, SQL-standard compliant DBMS on to a cloud storage system. In this field, the work co-authored [BFG+08] and supervised by [Pil12] Donald Kossmann are the single most related pieces of work.

In this work, we also focus on deploying a parallel DBMS on a cloud storage system, but (a) we keep all data resident in main memory all the time, (b) we apply a column-oriented data layout, and (c) we use the storage system for both—data access and code execution. This area of work in currently not addressed in the research community. Google works with Dremel in the same domain, but their approach is based on disk resident data. So far, the work co-authored [BFG+08] and supervised by [Pil12] Donald Kossmann, focuses on the processing of transactional workloads by a row-oriented database and it utilizes the cloud storage system solely as passive storage without considering the possibilities of operator shipping and execution.

Part I
A Database System Architecture for a
Shared Main Memory-Based Storage

Chapter 3
System Architecture

3.1 System Architecture—Requirements, Assumptions, and Overview

Requirements

In order to address the research questions as formulated in Sect. 1.2, we have to define a system architecture that meets the following requirements:

1. The overall system architecture is composed of a parallel DBMS and a storage system, following the principles of a shared-storage approach (as explained in Sect. 2.3.1) resulting in:

   a. A separation of the processors belonging to the parallel DBMS and the storage system with the processors sharing common access to the data inside the storage system.
   b. Each processor can access all data.
   c. The capacities of the parallel DBMS as well as the storage system can be adjusted independently.

2. The architecture of the parallel DBMS must support:

   a. Operating on data that is structured according to the relational model and process SQL-standard conform queries (as explained in Sect. 2.2).
   b. Organizing data in a columnar format (as explained in Sect. 2.2.1) and providing corresponding database operators which are able to execute workloads which benefit from column-oriented data (as explained in Sect. 2.2.2).
   c. Seamlessly switching between executing a database operator by itself or delegating the execution to someone else (as explained in Sect. 2.3.4).

3. The storage system is required to:

   a. Keep all data resident in main memory (as explained in Sect. 2.3.1).
   b. Provide durability, high-availability, scale gracefully, and be elastic (as explained in Sect. 2.4).

© Springer International Publishing Switzerland 2016
C. Tinnefeld, *Building a Columnar Database on RAMCloud*, In-Memory
Data Management Research, DOI 10.1007/978-3-319-20711-7_3

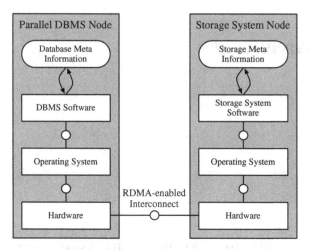

Fig. 3.1 Assumptions with regards to the deployed hardware and software stacks

    c. Provide data access as well as the possibility to execute code (as explained in Sect. 2.3.3).

4. The different components of the architecture are connected via a network infrastructure that supports remote direct memory access (RDMA) (as explained in Sect. 2.1.3).

Assumptions and Overview

The previously mentioned requirements can be addressed in many different ways. As discussed in Sects. 2.3.2 and 2.4.1, there are a number of state-of-the-art systems where each addresses a subset of the requirements. Utilizing them for constructing our architecture introduces a set of assumptions which we want to articulate in order to illustrate the translation from the requirements to the actual system architecture.

We make the following assumptions about our system architecture: the parallel DBMS runs on a number of servers which are referred to as nodes. Each node is equipped with its own hardware consisting of standard server hardware (as explained in Sect. 2.1) and a RDMA-enabled network interface card (as illustrated in Fig. 3.1[1]). The node is equipped with its own local storage in the form of a disk or SSD, but this is only used for storing the operating system and the DBMS software, but not parts of the database itself. Each node runs an instance of the parallel DBMS software and has access to meta information about the database such as the contained relations, attributes, data types, and foreign keys. The parallel DBMS is equipped with a central instance called a federator which accepts queries from clients and distributes them in a round-robin manner among the nodes in the parallel DBMS cluster. The number of nodes for the parallel DBMS can be adjusted in order to meet certain performance requirements.

---

[1]The Fundamental Modeling Concepts (FMC) notation [KGT06] is being used for architectural figures throughout this chapter.

The storage system also runs on its own servers which are referred to as nodes. Again, each node is equipped with its own hardware consisting of standard server hardware (as explained in Sect. 2.1) and an RDMA-enabled network interface card. Each node keeps all to-be-stored data resident in main memory, which implies that the overall storage capacity of the storage system cannot be greater than the sum of the main memories of all nodes. Each node utilizes a local disk or SSD to store also data in a non-volatile manner. For data recovery purposes, for example in the case of a failure of an individual node, the to-be-stored data is replicated and scattered across all nodes and can be recovered in a very short period of time. Each node runs the storage system software, which can access the storage meta information that describes the data it holds. The distribution of data and their replication across the nodes is managed by a central instance in the storage system. This central instance also distributes the information.

In this work, we use AnalyticsDB as parallel DBMS and Stanford's RAMCloud as storage system, and utilize them as components to construct the aforementioned

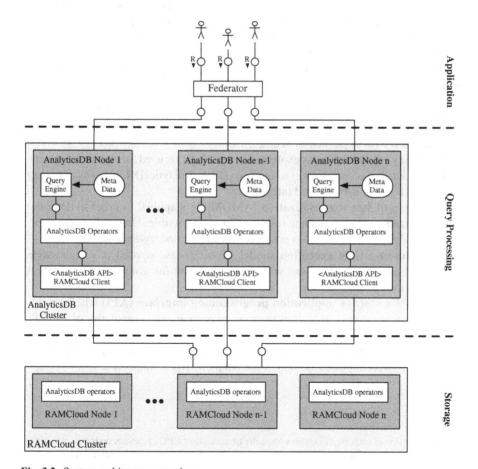

Fig. 3.2 System architecture overview

system architecture as illustrated in the system architecture overview in Fig. 3.2. Both components in combination allow fulfilling the previously stated requirements and go along with our assumptions as their detailed description in the remainder of this chapter shows.

3.2 AnalyticsDB

AnalyticsDB is our prototypical in-memory DBMS written in C++. It has been designed and developed in the context of this work. Initially, the idea was to stand on the shoulder of giants and utilize existing open-source in-memory columnar database systems and their implementations such as MonetDB [BKM08b] and HYRISE [GKP+10]: this option turned out to be cumbersome, since the operator execution in both systems is parameterized by providing the local memory address of the to be processed data. This makes the decoupling of operator execution and data location—and in turn the switching between operator execution on local or remote memory—difficult. Instead of reengineering those existing systems, AnalyticsDB has been designed and built from scratch.

The AnalyticsDB architecture is shown in Fig. 3.3 and features the following properties:

- A **columnar data layout** according to the decomposed storage model (as explained in Sect. 2.2.1) in combination with all **data residing permanently in main physical memory** (as explained in Sect. 2.2).
- **Dictionary compression** (as explained in Sect. 2.2.1) is used for compressing non-numeric attributes (e.g. string) to integer values. AnalyticsDB supports choosing between 2-, 4- or 8-byte sized integers.
- The pattern of **late materialization** [AMDM07] is applied in order to defer the materialization of intermediate results as long as possible. Until full materialization, AnalyticsDB operates on position lists and dictionary-encoded values.
- A **column-at-a-time execution model** [Bon02]—as opposed a Volcano-style [Gra94a] query execution—but without the policy of full column materialization (see previous point).
- The use of a **storage application programming interface (API)** which encapsulates storage access as well as operator execution. The granularity of the API is per column. This API can be implemented by using a local data structure or for example, using the client of a separate storage system.[2] Listing 3.1 shows an excerpt from a simplified version of the AnalyticsDB storage API.

---

[2]The introduction of such an API creates a penalty of a couple of CPU cycles per operator execution. However, since the ultimate goal is the evaluation of local versus remote operator execution this penalty is negligible.

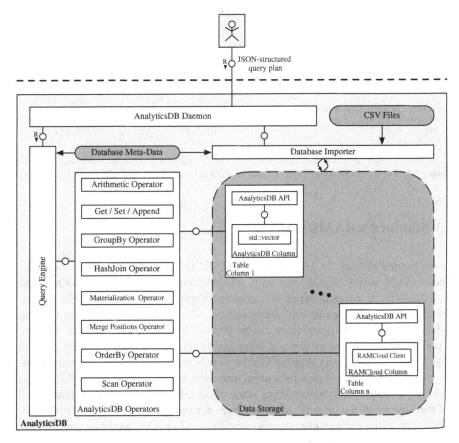

Fig. 3.3 AnalyticsDB architecture

- AnalyticsDB is designed to process queries written in **standard-compliant SQL**. The implementation in its current version accepts fully phrased query plans.
- AnalyticsDB can process **analytical and mixed workloads** (as explained in Sect. 2.2.2). The execution of mixed workloads is supported by **column-level locking** resulting in a **read committed isolation level**. In a distributed setup, one AnalyticsDB node handles all write operations while read-only operations can be executed by all remaining nodes[3]: this approach is common for scaling out an in-memory database system that handles a mixed workload as practiced for scaling-out HyPer [MRR+13] or by SAP HANA [LKF+13].

---

[3]As mentioned in Sect. 1.2, distributed transaction processing is out of scope in this work.

```
1  ColumnPosition  append(ColumnValue value);
   ColumnValue     get(ColumnPosition position);
   void            set(ColumnPosition position, ColumnValue value)
     ;

6  ColumnPositionList      scan(SCAN_COMPARATOR comparator,
                                ColumnValue value,
                                ColumnPositionList positionList);
   Array<ColumnValue> materialize(ColumnPositionList positionList);
   ColumnPositionList  joinProbe(ArrayRef probingValues,
11                               ColumnPositionList positionList);
   size_t size();
   void restore(ArrayRef values);
```

Listing 3.1 Excerpt from a simplified version of the AnalyticsDB storage API

3.3 Stanford's RAMCloud

As mentioned in Sect. 2.4.1, RAMCloud [OAE+11] is a storage system that combines DRAM-based data storage with a RDMA-enabled network. A RAMCloud consists of three different types of software components: a coordinator, a master, and a backup. Instances thereof are deployed on nodes of a RAMCloud whereat instances of different components can be deployed on the same physical machine at the same time. A master stores a set of objects in main memory, replicates these objects and corresponding changes synchronously over network into the main memory of a number of backups which asynchronously persist the data on disk/SSD. In addition, a central coordinator keeps track of all master and backup instances and the partitioning of the objects' address ranges across the different master instances. Clients can utilize the provided storage capabilities of a RAMCloud by using a RAMCloud library which enables them to communicate with the central coordinator and the master instances.

A coordinator is a central instance in RAMCloud as it maintains a global view on the locations of stored objects and the available master and backup servers. For doing so, it employs two different data structures: a tablet map which keeps track of the address ranges of stored objects, and the corresponding master that stores the objects within a certain address range, and a host list that keeps track of the locations of the different servers, their IP address, and their status. The coordinator is contacted by other entities to find out which master stores a certain object.

Each master stores a number of objects. The address range of all objects to be stored—as maintained in the tablet map of the coordinator—is partitioned among the different masters, where each master is considered as the owner of all objects that fall into a certain span of the global address range. Each master is responsible for populating updates on its objects to the corresponding backup servers. A master uses two different data structures to store its objects: a log-based data structure that stores the actual objects and an object map that keeps track of which object is placed at what position in the log. The look-up of an object has a complexity of $O(1)$ since the object map uses a hash function to look up the position of an object (Fig. 3.4).

Chapter 4
Data Storage

4.1 Mapping from Columnar Data to RAMCloud Objects

Using RAMCloud with its key-value based data model as storage system for a columnar DBMS results in the question how to map the columnar data to objects in RAMCloud. RAMCloud provides the concept of namespaces. A namespace defines a logical container for a set of objects, where each object key occurs only once. Upon the creation of a new namespace, the parameter *server span* is set to define how many storage nodes will be used to store the objects of the namespace. These namespaces are assigned to nodes in a round-robin manner. Assignment of key-value pairs across nodes is done by partitioning the range of the hashes of the object keys contained in that namespace.

To map an AnalyticsDB table, we create a namespace for each database table attribute with the naming convention "*dbname::dbtablename::attributename*". In each namespace we create a number of objects, while each object stores a chunk of the corresponding attribute column. How many column values are held by a single object is configurable via a parameter *object size*. The object size parameter and the actual size of the column determine how many objects have to be created for storing the complete column. Figure 4.1 depicts this concept for a table consisting of two columns *id* and *name* with *object size*=3. We discuss the importance and determination of the *object size* parameter in the next section. To store the complete example table, we create a namespace for each attribute and create three objects with keys 0–2 for every column. In the example depicted in Fig. 4.1, we define *server span=3* for namespace "*db1::cust:id*" and "*db1:cust:name*" resulting in the shown distribution for a three node RAMCloud cluster.

Putting this partitioning mechanism in context with the aforementioned data mapping has the following implication: the partition granularity is on AnalyticsDB column level, meaning it is not possible to enforce placing an entire AnalyticsDB table consisting of several columns on a single RAMCloud storage node (except when the RAMCloud cluster has only one node).

© Springer International Publishing Switzerland 2016
C. Tinnefeld, *Building a Columnar Database on RAMCloud*, In-Memory
Data Management Research, DOI 10.1007/978-3-319-20711-7_4

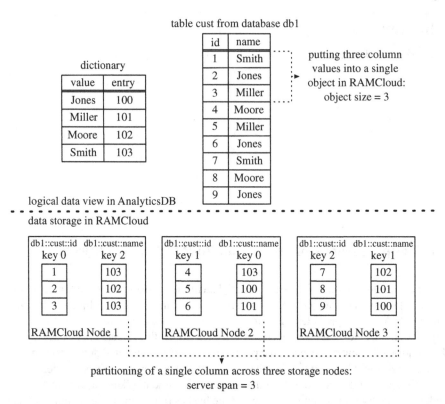

Fig. 4.1 Mapping from AnalyticsDB columns to objects in RAMCloud. Partitioning of two columns across four storage nodes with a server span=3

4.2 Main Memory Access Costs and Object Sizing

The introduction of splitting columnar data to key-value pairs raises the question if it ruins the advantages of columnar data storage? As explained in Sect. 2.2.1, the sequential data alignment of columnar data placement in main memory allows exploiting cache and spatial locality: we have to clarify if chopping the columnar data into small key-value pairs lets these advantages vanish and how much data has to be held sequentially to enable the advantages of columnar data storage? In order to address those questions we a) formally describe main memory access costs in dependence of the size and sequential alignment of the to be accessed data and b) present a set of corresponding experiments and micro-benchmarks. The foundation for our formal description is the generic database cost models for hierarchical memory systems from Manegold et al. [MBK02b, MBK02c] that we extend by a data access pattern that represents our problem.

In the model from Manegold et al., the multiple cascading levels of cache memories between the main memory and the CPU are referred to as individual caches

(Level 1 Cache, Level 2 Cache etc.) and are denoted in this work with a subscript i. Caches are characterized by three major characteristics: the capacity C defines the total capacity of a cache in bytes, the cache line or cache block size B describes the smallest unit of transfer between adjacent cache levels, and the cache associativity A influences the cache replacement policy. Additionally, the cache latency l describes the time span (in CPU cycles or in nanoseconds (ns)) that passes between requesting data and having it available. The bandwidth b is a metric that notes the data volume (in megabytes per seconds (MB/s)) that can be transferred between two levels of the hierarchy within a certain period of time. When it comes to measuring the latency and the bandwidth, there is a distinction between sequential and random access due to Extended Data Output (EDO). Another relevant concept is address translation which is used to translate virtual memory addresses to physical page address. The Translation Lookaside Buffer (TLB) holds the most recently used pages and is treated as another layer in the memory hierarchy. As a summary, the aforementioned cache parameters are listed in Table 4.1.

Data Access Patterns and Their Costs
The total time T needed for a computing task that works on data persisted in main memory can be expressed by the sum of the needed CPU time T_{CPU} and the corresponding memory access time T_{Mem}.

$$T = T_{CPU} + T_{Mem} \qquad (4.1)$$

Deriving T_{CPU} is straightforward as it is the pure CPU time that is needed once the data has traveled through the memory hierarchies to the CPU. Modeling T_{Mem} is more sophisticated, though, as it has to take the memory hierarchies and the different latencies associated with the respective access patterns into consideration.

Table 4.1 Overview on cache parameters ($i \in \{1, \ldots, N\}$)[3] (taken from [MBK02b])

Description	Unit	Symbol
Cache name (level)	–	L_i
Cache capacity	[bytes]	C_i
Cache block size	[bytes]	B_i
Number of cache lines	–	$\#_i = C_i/B_i$
Cache associativity	–	A_i
Sequential access		
Access bandwidth	[bytes/ns]	b^s_{i+1}
Access latency	[ns]	$l^s_{i+1} = B_i/b^s_{i+1}$
Random access		
Access latency	[ns]	l^r_{i+1}
Access bandwidth	[bytes/ns]	$b^r_{i+1} = B_i/l^r_{i+1}$

$$T_{Mem} = \sum_{i=1}^{N} (M_i^s \cdot l_{i+1}^s + M_i^r \cdot l_{i+1}^r) \tag{4.2}$$

As shown in Eq. (4.2), the memory access time is modeled by adding the product of the sequential cache misses M^s, and the sequential access latency l^s, and the product of the random cache misses M^r and random access latency l^r. This is done for all memory hierarchies i independently, whereat the latency always describes the latency needed for accessing the next memory hierarchy. In order to be able to apply this model, Manegold et al. introduced a unified description of data structures referred to as data regions and the corresponding data operations thereupon which are referred to as data access patterns.

A data region R consists of $R.n$ data items where each data item has a size of $R.w$ bytes. Consequently, the product $R.n \cdot R.w$ expresses the size $||R||$ of a data region R. A data region R spans $|R|_B$ cache lines and $|C|_{R.w}$ data items fit in the cache. A tuple u specifies how many bytes are actually used out of every data region $R.n$ (e.g. if all bytes are used then u equals $R.n$). We extend the description of a data region by adding the concept of a block where a data region R consists of $Blk.n$ blocks and each block covers $Blk.w$ data items, as illustrated in Fig. 4.2. The product $Blk.n \cdot Blk.w$ equals $R.n$.

Data access patterns describe the different ways of sweeping over data and vary in their referential locality. Therefore, not only the access latency and the resulting costs per cache miss, but also the number of cache misses differ between access patterns. Cache misses can be divided into random and sequential misses, the different associated costs depend on the performance optimization features of the underlying hardware. A sequential miss is a miss of data which is closely located to the previously read data, whereas a random miss describes accessing data which is not closely located to the previously accessed data. A random miss always causes the full costs of memory access, whereat a sequential miss can benefit from hardware that exploits data locality. Based on the two different kinds of cache misses, Manegold et al. [MBK02b] introduced different data access patterns. Consecutively, we describe the two most relevant—namely the single sequential traversal and the single random traversal—and then introduce the single random block traversal pattern.

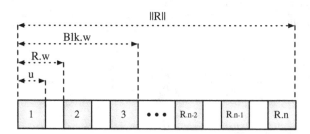

Fig. 4.2 Illustration of data region R

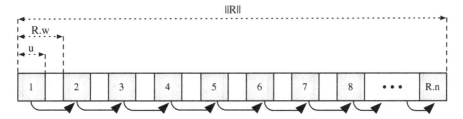

Fig. 4.3 Single sequential traversal access pattern (taken from [MBK02b])

Single Sequential Traversal. As illustrated in Fig. 4.3, a single sequential traversal $s\_tra(R[, u])$ accesses $R.n$ data items in a data region R. It does so by processing the data items in the same order as they are stored in memory. Hence, a single sequential traversal produces exactly one random miss which is the first access. After that, it reads or writes u consecutive bytes out of every data item $R.n$. Consequently, if the length $R.w$ of a data item equals u, then the whole data item gets loaded. If u is smaller than $R.w$, a constant part is skipped between two values which is defined by $R.w - u$. When describing the costs T_{Mem} associated with a single sequential traversal within a data region R, it is essential to differentiate if the gap $R.w - u$ between two adjacent accesses is smaller or greater than or equal to the size B of a single cache line. If the gap is smaller, each loaded cache line serves at least one adjacent access. Consequently, when going over data region R, all covered cache lines B have to be loaded as modeled in Eq. 4.3.

$$M_i^s(s\_tra^s(R, u)) = |R|_{B_i} \tag{4.3}$$

If the gap between two adjacent accesses is greater than or equal to a single cache line, not all cache lines covered by R have to be loaded. Additionally, if a tuple u is not placed in correspondence with the cache line size, reading or writing it could result in the necessity to load two separate cache lines. Taking both additional constraints into account, the costs can be modeled as noted in Eq. 4.4.

$$M_i^s(s\_tra^s(R, u)) = R.n \cdot \left(\left\lceil \frac{u}{B_i} \right\rceil + \frac{(u - 1) \bmod B_i}{B_i} \right) \tag{4.4}$$

Single Random Traversal. As illustrated in Fig. 4.4, a single random traversal $r\_tra(R[, u])$ accesses each data item $R.n$ in R exactly once, whereas the data items not accessed in the sequence are stored in memory, but completely at random. Out of every data item $R.n$, u consecutive bytes are read or written. A single random traversal does not produce any sequential misses. The memory costs associated with a single random traversal $r\_tra(R[, u])$ depend again on the size of the gap $R.w - u$ between two adjacent accesses. If the gap is equal or larger to the size B of a single cache line, then no adjacent access can benefit from an already loaded cache line, which makes the same formula applicable as for the single sequential traversal in such a case (see Eq. 4.5).

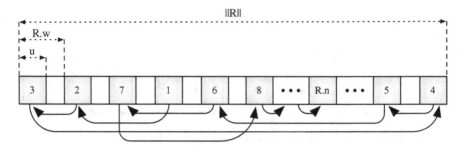

Fig. 4.4 Single random traversal access pattern (taken from [MBK02b])

$$M_i^r(r\_tra^r(R,u)) = R.n \cdot \left(\left\lceil \frac{u}{B_i} \right\rceil + \frac{(u-1)\bmod B_i}{B_i} \right) \tag{4.5}$$

If the gap between two adjacent accesses is smaller than a single cache line, a single cache line may have to be loaded several times throughout the sweep, as locally adjacent data is not accessed in the same order. As it is possible that a cache line has been purged out of the cache before all accesses to it are completed, the probability of an early eviction has to be modeled. The likelihood of an early eviction depends on $\|R\|$ and the cache capacity C. As an eviction only occurs once, the available cache capacity is filled, the number $\#_i$ of cache lines that can be stored in the cache—and in case of having tuple that spans several cache lines—the number of data items $R.w$ that fit into cache are of relevance. Putting it all together, the cache misses can be derived by applying Eq. 4.6 below.

$$M_i^r(r\_tra^r(R,u)) = |R|_{B_i} +$$
$$(R.n - \min\{\#_i, |C_i|_{R.w}\}) \cdot \left(1 - min\left\{1, \frac{C_i}{\|R\|}\right\}\right) \tag{4.6}$$

Single Random Block Traversal. We define a single random block traversal $rb\_tra(Blk, R[, u])$ as a sweep over a data region R where every data item $R.n$ in R is accessed exactly once, whereas the data items are grouped in $Blk.n$ blocks. Within each block the data items are traversed sequentially, however the blocks themselves are randomly placed in the memory. Hence, a single random block traversal starts with a random access in order to get the first data item of the first block, followed by a number of sequential accesses depending on the number of data items $Blk.w$ per block, followed again by a random access for retrieving the first data item out of the next block. This implies the following two extreme cases: if $Blk.w$ equals $R.n$ and all data items are stored in one single block, the sweep equals a single sequential traversal and the resulting cache misses can be described through the Eqs. 4.3 and 4.4. In contrast, if $Blk.w$ equals $R.w$ and each block contains just a single data item, the sweep equals a single random traversal and the resulting cache misses can be described through the Eqs. 4.5 and 4.6 (Fig. 4.5).

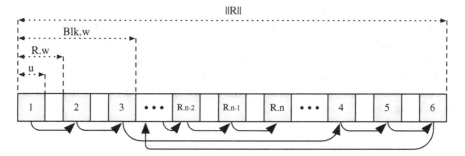

Fig. 4.5 Single random block traversal access pattern

Disregarding the extreme cases, one can observe that the block sizing influences the ratio of random and sequential misses. When describing the random access for retrieving the first data item out of each block, one can differentiate if the block size $Blk.w$ is greater than or equal to or smaller than the size B of a single cache line. If the block size is greater than or equal, a distinct cache line has to be touched for every block $Blk.n$ in R. Hence, the number of cache misses per cache hierarchy level equals the number of blocks, as shown in Eq. 4.7.

$$M_i^r(rb\_tra^r(Blk, R, u)) = Blk.n_i \qquad (4.7)$$

If the block size is smaller than a cache line, again we have at least as many cache misses as we have blocks. Additionally, there is the chance that a cache line has to be accessed several times, as it stores two or more disjunct blocks, but since locally adjacent access is not temporally adjacent, the cache line must be loaded again into the cache for every block access in a worst case scenario. Consequently, depending on block sizing and cache capacity, each access to a different block which is stored in the same cache line may result in an additional cache miss as described in Eq. 4.8.

$$M_i^r(rb\_tra^r(Blk, R, u)) = Blk.n +$$
$$(Blk.n - \min\{\#_i, |C_i|_{Blk.w}\}) \cdot \left(1 - min\left\{1, \frac{C_i}{||R||}\right\}\right) \qquad (4.8)$$

The sequential access in the context of the single random block traversal covers the sequential sweep over the remaining $Blk.w - 1$ data items in every block. Having a block size $Blk.w$ smaller than the cache line size B also implies that the gap $R.w - u$ between two data items is smaller than B and all cache lines covering the remaining data items have to be loaded as noted in Eq. 4.9. This equation is also applicable if the block size $Blk.w$ is larger than B, but the gaps between two data items are still smaller than B.

$$M_i^s(rb\_tra^s(Blk, R, u)) = |Blk_n \cdot (Blk_w - 1)|_{B_i} \qquad (4.9)$$

If the block size *Blk.w* as well as the gap *R.w* − *u* is bigger than or equal to the cache line size *B*, not all cache lines covered by a block have to be loaded. Similar to a single sequential traversal, a suboptimal placement of a tuple *u* can result in accessing separate cache lines. The resulting number of cache misses is the product of the number of remaining data items per block over all blocks and the occurrence of cache misses in correspondence with the tuple size *u* and the cache line size B_i as shown in Eq. 4.10.

$$M_i^s(rb\_tra^s(Blk, R, u)) =$$
$$(Blk_n \cdot (Blk_w - 1)) \cdot \left(\left\lceil \frac{u}{B_i} \right\rceil + \frac{(u - 1) \, \text{mode} \, B_i}{B_i} \right) \quad (4.10)$$

Experiments

After formally describing the occurring cache misses when traversing block-wise grouped data in main memory, we present a set of experiments. Through the experiments we want to gain insights to what extent bandwidth-bound operations can be accelerated by a block-wise grouping of data, and in the correlation between data item and block size.

The experiments are based on a prototypical implementation of a hashtable which can be partitioned into blocks. When initializing the hashtable, one can define the size of a block which implicitly determines into how many blocks the hashtable will be partitioned. If the block size is chosen to equal a single data item, the block mechanism has no further impact, as all data items will be placed randomly—according to the hash value of their key—within in the hashtable. An IBM Blade-Server H21 XM with a Intel Xeon E5450 CPU (the CPU has a L1 cache capacity of 32 KB, a L2 cache capacity of 6 MB, and a L1 + L2 cache line size of 64 bytes) was used for the experiments.

The experiment executes a data traversal which touches 10 million data items in total—such an operation underlies a scan operation in AnalyticsDB. Throughout the experiments we vary three different factors: the data item size *R.w*, the block size *Blk.w*, and the type of operation on the data. The data item size *R.w* is set to 16,64, or 1024 bytes in order to have data items which are smaller than the L1 or L2 data cache size as well as significantly bigger than both. The block size or the number of consecutive data items per block are increased in steps throughout the experiments. The data that is used in the experiments has the following characteristics: each data item consists of at least of one integer value making the minimum size of a data item 4 bytes. This integer value is the only data that is actually touched during our experiments and is therefore *u*. Consequently, data items with a size *R.w* of 16, 64 or 1024 bytes have all the same 4 byte *u*, but they vary in their padding. The padding is done with additional integer, boolean, and string values. In every experiment run, 10 millions of such data items are traversed. Consequently, the size ||*R*|| of the data region is 153, 610, or 9766 megabytes depending on whether the data item size *R.w* is set to 16, 64, or 1024 bytes.

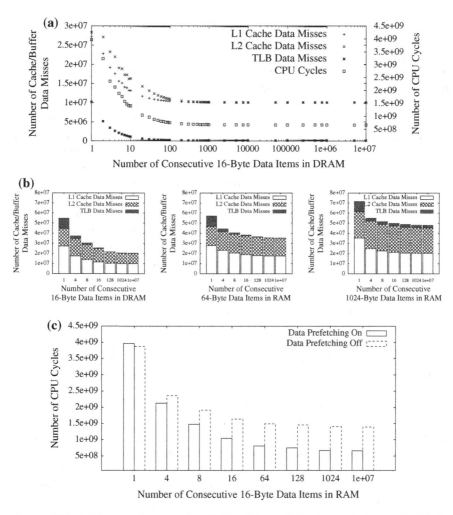

Fig. 4.6 Object sizing experiments. **a** Detailed breakdown of data traversal with varying block size ($Blk.w = \{1, 10, 100, 1000, 10000, 10^6, 10^7\}R.n$, **b** data traversal with varying data item ($R.w = \{16, 64, 1024\}Bytes$) and block size ($Blk.w = \{1, 4, 8, 16, 128, 1024, 10^7\}R.n$), **c** impact of prefetching and block sizing on CPU cycles spent for data traversal

Figure 4.6b illustrates the number of L1 and L2 cache data and TLB misses during the data traversal. The three graphs vary in the data item size $R.w$ (16,64,1024 bytes). When having a data item size of 16 bytes, one can observe that the number of L1 cache data misses is reduced by 50 %, the number of L2 cache misses is reduced by 13 %, and the number of TLB misses is reduced by 86 % when eight data items are grouped in a block compared to one data item per block ($Blk.w = 8$ vs $Blk.w = 1$). When having a data item size of 64 bytes, one can observe that the number of L1 cache data misses is reduced by 27 %, the number of L2 cache misses remains constant, and the number of TLB misses is reduced by 86 % when eight data items are grouped in a block compared to one data item per block. When having a data item size of 1024 bytes, one can observe that the number of L1 cache data misses is reduced by 36 %, the number of L2 cache misses remains constant, and the number of TLB misses is reduced by 74 % when eight data items are grouped in a block compared to one data item per block. Although the exact numbers vary, one can see a similar drop in cache misses during the disaggregation task, once the block size is increased. Additionally, one can observe that at a block size of around 128 data items, the minimum number of cache misses for all hierarchy levels is reached. This observation matches with Fig. 4.6a.

The calculations and experiments so far have been made with activated data prefetching as it is the CPU chipset's default mode. As indicated in Sect. 2.2.1, prefetching has an impact on sequential data traversal. In this paragraph, we want to experimentally quantify that impact. Figure 4.6c compares the needed CPU cycles for executing the data traversal with a data item size $R.w$ of 16 bytes, and with activated and deactivated data prefetching. One can see that the bigger the block size is set, the more performance improvements can be achieved. Starting from a block size with 128 data items, activated prefetching can speed-up the aggregation task by a factor two. Figure 4.6c shows that for a block size $Blk.w = 1$, the execution with deactivated prefetching is actually faster. This is due to incorrect prefetching which describes the blocking of the memory and the bus for fetching the next adjacent cache line. Yet this cache line will not be used, as all values are placed randomly in memory, but while it is prefetched, the transmission of the correct cache line is prevented.

In conclusion, the micro benchmarks in Fig. 4.6 illustrate that the required number of CPU cycles becomes minimal if a relatively small amount of data items are placed consecutively in DRAM and, therefore, the maximum data traversal or scan speed has already been reached. In the shown micro benchmarks a block size of around 1000 data items is sufficient to reach the maximum data traversal speed. Reflecting these insights on the object sizing in RAMCloud, we choose the allowed upper limit of 1MB for RAMCloud objects which results in an object size of 131.072 (as an AnalyticsDB column value is 8 bytes). Given the results of our benchmark above, we conclude that we still achieve maximum scan performance with this partitioning schema, which is validated in the subsequent Chap. 6 with a scan operation micro benchmark shown in Fig. 6.1a.

Chapter 5
Data Processing

5.1 Database Operators in AnalyticsDB

AnalyticsDB processes queries with the help of eight different database operators. Each database operator O accepts as input a single or several column(s) C and/or (a) position list(s) P. Each operator O evaluates a condition D and outputs a single value or column(s) or a position list. A position list can be seen as a filter on a column, as it references a subset of the total entries in a column. Since AnalyticsDB applies the pattern of late materialization (see Sect. 3.2), it tries to work with position lists as long as possible during the processing of a query for performance improvements. Table 5.1 presents an overview of the operators. Although the table shows that most operators accept one or more columns as input, they also accept a position list as input if the to be processed column is not materialized yet. Similar to the input, the output can also be a materialized column or just a position list. A database table from an operator's perspective is just a collection of columns.

The Arithmetic Operator allows mathematical operations such as addition, subtraction, multiplication, or division between the tuples of two columns. The GroupBy Operator can reduce a table by a certain criteria which is denoted by the GroupBy Columns. The reduction is done by aggregating the corresponding tuples in the aggregation column, for example, by calculating the sum. After the execution of a GroupBy operation, only the distinct combinations of the particular GroupBy Columns are being returned. A HashJoin Operation identifies the matching tuples of two or more columns. If two tuples are considered to match is defined via the join criteria which can express that the two tuples e.g. should have the same value. The HashJoin Operation utilizes a hash table as an auxiliary data structure for executing the join by inserting the tuples from one column into the hash table, and then probing with each value from the other relation. The Materialize Operator accepts as input a position list and a column, and returns the tuples as specified in the position list. The Merge Position List Operator merges two or more position lists. The OrderBy Operator sorts by (a) to be specified OrderBy Column(s), and the tuples of additional columns are rearranged accordingly. A Scan Operator traverses a column and evaluates for each

© Springer International Publishing Switzerland 2016

C. Tinnefeld, *Building a Columnar Database on RAMCloud*, In-Memory
Data Management Research, DOI 10.1007/978-3-319-20711-7_5

Table 5.1 Database Operators in AnalyticsDB

Operator	Input		Output
Arithmetic	Columns	Operation (add, sub, mult, div)	Column
GroupBy	Column(s)	Aggregation Column Type (sum, average, count) GroupBy Column(s)	Column(s)
HashJoin	Columns	Join Criteria	Column(s) or Position List
Materialize	Column	Position List	Column
Merge Position Lists	Position Lists	——-	Position List
OrderBy	Column(s)	OrderBy Column(s)	Table
Scan	Column	Operand(s) Comparator(s) $(>, \geq, =, \leq, <)$ Logical Combination $(\&, \|)$	Column or Position List

tuple if a condition matches. This condition can contain one or two operand(s), one or two comparator(s), and a logical combination.

5.2 Operator Push-Down into RAMCloud

So far we have described how RAMCloud is used as shared storage in our system. With a standard configuration of RAMCloud, query execution can only happen on an AnalyticsDB node by loading the required data from RAMCloud into the query processing engine of an AnalyticsDB node. In this section we describe how we extend the RAMCloud system to allow for execution of database operators directly in the storage close to the data. Specifically, we first identify which operators are most significant for a database system designed for read-mostly workloads, such as AnalyticsDB, and then describe how we designed and implemented these operators in RAMCloud.

We analyze the queries of the Star-Schema-Benchmark (SSB) [O'N] to identify which operators benefit from a push-down into the storage system. Table 5.2 shows the AnalyticsDB operator break-down for one execution cycle of the SSB with a sizing factor of 10 in local main memory on an Intel Xeon E5620. The complete execution time is normalized to highlight the contribution of each operator to the total execution time. To identify operators which should be considered for a push-down, two questions are of interest: to what extent does an operator contribute to the overall execution time? Does the operator usually work on data as stored in the storage system or on intermediate results?

Table 5.2 AnalyticsDB operator break-down when executing the Star Schema Benchmark, normalized by the contribution of the operator to the overall query runtime

	Arithmetic	GroupBy	Hash-Join	Materialize	Merge Positions	OrderBy	Scan
%	0.0003	0.0754	0.6657	0.0693	0.0283	0.001	0.1594

Table 5.2 shows that the Hash-Join and Scan operator accumulate 82 % of the total execution time in the SSB. From our query execution plans for the SSB, we derived that these operators are always the first to touch the raw data and consume it sequentially. The Materialization Operator also works directly on the data as stored in the persistence, for example when retrieving the actual values in a column based on a position list. Consequently, we decided to implement support for these operators in the storage layer.

As a first approach, we want to push-down the execution of operators which operate *on one relation at a time*. This simplifies the push-down, as it avoids the synchronization of two separate operator executions in the storage system. However, the HashJoin Operator works on two or more relations at a time, and in order to supports its execution in the storage system, we dissect its execution into three parts ($S \bowtie R$ with $S <= R$): building the hash table from relation S (hashBuild), probing against relation R (joinProbe), and optionally materializing the tuples that meet the join condition (materialize). Pushing down the execution of the hashBuild seems impractical as (a) each RAMCloud node sees only a fraction of the data which would introduce the extra effort to merge the different hash tables and (b) the execution of this merge operation in RAMCloud would require additional synchronization. Therefore, it is favorable to send the data from relation S to the AnalyticsDB node and build the hash table there. Instead the join probing is eligible for a push-down, as each probing operation can happen separately at each respective RAMCloud node. The same applies to a potentially subsequent materialization operation. Consequently, we added support for the *Scan, Materialization*, and *JoinProbing* operation in RAMCloud. The Group-By, Merge Position Lists, Sort, and Arithmetic operators work mostly on intermediate results which are processed inside the query engine of an AnalyticsDB node and, therefore, are not eligible for being pushed down to RAMCloud.

5.3   From SQL Statement to Main Memory Access

To allow for the push-down of the Scan and Materialization Operators as well as Join-Probing to RAMCloud nodes, we implement support for these operators in RAMCloud and add their operator signatures to the AnalyticsDB storage API as shown in Listing 3.1. To implement the AnalyticsDB storage API for RAMCloud, we added the corresponding RAMCloud client code in AnalyticsDB for invoking the operators in RAMCloud. The RAMCloud client component is responsible for mapping the columnar data to RAMCloud namespaces and objects.

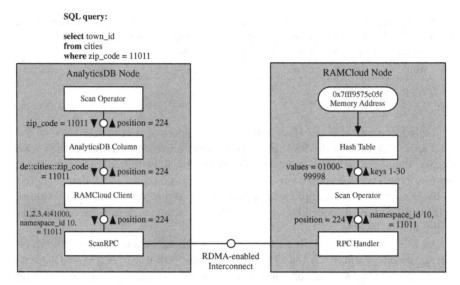

Fig. 5.1 From SQL statement in AnalyticsDB to the corresponding main memory access in RAMCloud

Figure 5.1 illustrates how the processing of a SQL query in an AnalyticsDB node results in a main memory access in a RAMCloud node. The presented query includes the execution of a Scan Operator which scans through the column zip code and aims to find tuples whose value equals 11011. The Scan Operator is executed on the respective AnalyticsDB column which then invokes the RAMCloud client: the invocation passes the fully qualified namespace of the column in RAMCloud as well as the scan operand. The RAMCloud client maps the namespace to a RAMCloud namespace ID (called RAMCloud internally tablet, see Sect. 3.3) and in our example the data belonging to this namespace sits on a single RAMCloud node. The RAMCloud client also resolves the corresponding IP address and port, and invokes a SCAN remote procedure call (RPC). The incoming RPC is handled by a RPC handler in the RAM-Cloud node which passes the to-be-scanned namespace id and the scan operand to its Scan Operator. The Scan Operator reads the key-value pairs which belong to this namespace from the hash table: in our example there are 1000 column tuples stored per key-value pair. Since there are 30000 different zip codes in the zip code column (with the lowest value being 01000 and the highest 99998), the scan operator has to traverse 30 key value pairs and finds the zip code 11011 at the position 224. This position information is then passed back to AnalyticsDB. In a next step, the town id resolves to position 224 in the cities table.

Part II
Database Operator Execution on a Shared Main Memory-Based Storage

Chapter 6
Operator Execution on One Relation

In this chapter we introduce an execution cost model for AnalyticsDB to analyze the impact of different parameters that have been induced by the data mapping, column partitioning, and the design of the operators itself. We first derive an abstract system model which is later used to predict execution costs analytically for different scenarios. Afterwards, we use our cost model to evaluate operator push-down and data pull execution strategies and show how the cost model can be used to decide on different execution strategies. We start with operators that operate on one relation at a time, continuing with two or more relations in the next chapter.

Related System Models

There are a number of system models available that can be applied to model the operator execution costs in a parallel DBMS. For example, Culler et al. from University of California, Berkeley present LogP [CKP+93] as a step towards a realistic model of distributed and parallel computation. LogP intends to be a general model that can be applied in the context of portable and parallel algorithms. L defines the latency introduced by communicating a message, o identifies the overhead for transmitting and receiving a message, g defines the gap between consecutive message transmissions, and P describes the number of processor and memory modules. Although an approach as LogP is generally applicable, system models in the context of distributed query processing and database operator execution take additional query processing-related aspects into consideration. This is demonstrated by Lanzelotte et al. who present a cost model [LVZ93] for query execution in a parallel DBMS. They consider the number of tuples in a relation R, the size of one tuple of a relation R, the CPU and network speed, the size of a packet as well as the time needed for sending and receiving messages. Based on these input parameters, they define cost functions for the various database operations. Özsu and Valduriez [ÖV11] describe a cost model for the query optimizer for a parallel DBMS. They define the cost of a plan as three components: total work, response time, and memory consumption.

© Springer International Publishing Switzerland 2016
C. Tinnefeld, *Building a Columnar Database on RAMCloud*, In-Memory
Data Management Research, DOI 10.1007/978-3-319-20711-7_6

the data transfer over network and overhead costs such as merging the results from all nodes. We further explore this causality by executing a set of 42 scan operations on three different columns. The scan operations vary in their selectivity, the columns vary in their size (60 million values, 800,000 values, and 2556 values). We execute the scan operations multiple times, but vary across how many RAMCloud nodes each column is being partitioned (via the RAMCloud server span parameter as explained in Sect. 4.1). The variation includes storing each column on a single RAMCloud node (server span=1) up to partitioning each column across 20 RAMCloud nodes (server span=20). Figure 6.3 depicts the scan operations on the column with 60 million values benefit up to a factor 5 from being distributed, the scan operations on the column with 800,000 values get accelerated up to factor 1.6, but the scan operations performance on the column with 2556 values decreases with every additional node up to a factor 4.5.

So far, we have only covered the aspect of data partitioning when one AnalyticsDB instance operates exclusively on a RAMCloud cluster. Now we cover the aspect of partitioning in combination with a variable number of AnalyticsDB nodes: we have a constant number of 20 nodes in the RAMCloud cluster, but vary the number of AnalyticsDB nodes between 1 and 30. If a new AnalyticsDB node is added, it is instructed by the federator to continuously execute the SSB: this results in an load increase. Figure 6.4 shows the corresponding experiment: in Fig. 6.4a the server span is 10 and in Fig. 6.4b the server span is 20. In Fig. 6.4a the throughput increases until 15 AnalyticsDB nodes and then begins to flatten out, which means the operator throughput is saturated in RAMCloud. The maximum throughput is 2607 SSB cycles per hour. In Fig. 6.4b the throughput increases until 20 AnalyticsDB nodes and then begins to flatten out. The maximum throughout is 3280 SSB cycles per hour.

The following two insights can be derived from the experiments: (a) we demonstrated that a server span of 10 delivers the optimal SSB execution time when a single AnalyticsDB node uses a RAMCloud cluster with 20 nodes. This statement is valid

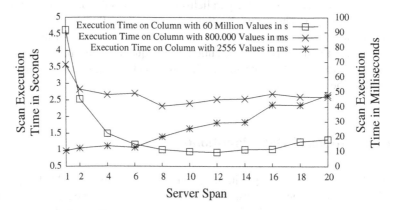

Fig. 6.3 AnalyticsDB runs on a single node with a operator push execution strategy, the RAMCloud cluster has a size of 20 nodes, the server span varies

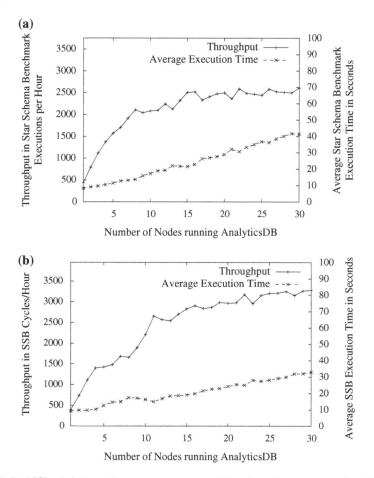

Fig. 6.4 RAMCloud cluster with a constant number of 20 nodes and a varying number (1–30) of nodes running AnalyticsDB with a operator push execution strategy and a Star Schema Benchmark data scale factor of 10. **a** RAMCloud running on 20 Nodes with Server Span=10, **b** RAMCloud running on 20 Nodes with Server Span=20

if there are up to ten AnalyticsDB nodes running. More than ten AnalyticsDB nodes per server span of 20 results in a better SSB execution time as the to-be-accessed data is distributed across more RAMCloud nodes and therefore the operator throughput in RAMCloud is saturated at a later point. (b) Even in the case of over-provisioning (e.g. 30 AnalyticsDB nodes vs. 20 RAMCloud nodes) the SSB throughput remains constant, but the execution time increases over linearly (due to the operator throughput saturation in RAMCloud), but it does not result in a reduction of the SSB throughput. In addition, the increasing throughput in both experiments can either be leveraged for performing a higher number of SSB executions in parallel or for reducing the execution time of a single SSB execution by dispatching its queries across the different AnalyticsDB nodes via the federator.

Chapter 7
Operator Execution on Two Relations

The previous Chapter describes the possibility of pushing-down the execution of database operators into RAMCloud, but the corresponding model is limited to operating on a single database column or relation at a time. This is practical for the execution of a scan operation, but necessitates breaking up a join operation into two separate operations. This comes along with the previously mentioned drawbacks of (a) limiting the maximum size of a join-relation by the client's available main memory and (b) bringing up the bottleneck of the client's network link. In addition, it makes pre- or post-join projections in the context of a join very expensive as the intermediate results always have to be transferred to the client instead of leaving them in the storage system. Motivated by avoiding those drawbacks, we describe in this chapter the execution and comparison of different distributed join algorithms inside RAMCloud.

Before we describe the choice of the to-be-evaluated join algorithms, we extend the existing system model and define the following assumptions with regards to the distributed join execution within RAMCloud: we execute a join operation between two relations $S \bowtie R$ with $S_{Size} <= R_{Size}$. The data of a relation is partitioned across a number of RAMCloud nodes ($n_{partR/S}$), but among those nodes the data distribution is considered to be even. As explained previously, the data from a relation is distributed on a fine granular level in a round-robin manner across the respective RAMCloud nodes. Consequently, we also assume that the data is partitioned evenly across the nodes even after filtering or a pre-join projection. For the execution of our models a pre-join projection results in a smaller S_{Size}/R_{Size}.

It is possible that a number of RAMCloud nodes hold some data from R as well as S ($n_{partOvl}$). The RAMCloud nodes used for executing the join (n_{join}) are either a sub- or superset of $n_{partR/S}$. In order to reduce the amount of data to be transferred, joins are executed as semi-joins which results in transferring only the join predicate containing relations, and is succeeded by a materialization of the remaining relations as defined by the query. However, this potentially necessary materialization is out of our scope as we define a join execution as finished when the matching tuples from both relations are derived across all RAMCloud nodes that executed the join (n_{join}).

© Springer International Publishing Switzerland 2016
C. Tinnefeld, *Building a Columnar Database on RAMCloud*, In-Memory
Data Management Research, DOI 10.1007/978-3-319-20711-7_7

Table 7.1 System model symbols for operating on two relations at a time

Symbol	Parameter
n	# of nodes in the cluster
R/S	To be joined relations R/S
n_{partR}	# of nodes relation R is partitioned across
n_{partS}	# of nodes relation S is partitioned across
$n_{partOvl}$	# of nodes where relations R and S overlap
n_{join}	# of nodes used for processing a join
$N_{1...i}^{partR/S}$	Individual nodes with a partition of R/S
$N_{1...i}^{join}$	Individual nodes used for processing a join
$|R|\,/\,|S|$	Individual records of R/S
$R_{1...i}/S_{1...i}$	Individual partitions of R/S
$|R_i|\,/\,|S_i|$	Individual records of a partition of R/S
R_{size}/S_{size}	Size of relations R/S in bytes
BW_{net}	Network throughput between two nodes in bytes/sec
BW_{hash}	In-memory throughput for building an hash table on a single node in bytes/sec
BW_{probe}	In-memory throughput for probing against an hash table on a single node in bytes/sec

Table 7.1 explains the parameters and their notation used within join algorithms and our analytical model.

There is a great variety of different join algorithms in the field of parallel database systems. However, when comparing the different algorithms, there are two aspects which strongly characterize such an algorithm: the way the data is partitioned and transferred across the participating nodes for the join execution, and the mechanism to perform the actual comparison between elements of the two join-relations on each node. Since we implement and execute the joins in a storage system with switched fabric communication links, we want to focus on the implications of data partitioning and transfer, and not on the different options for performing the data item comparisons. Therefore, we only consider hashing and probing for the comparison (and not e.g. sort-merge), since it is a well-established technique, especially in the context of main memory data access [BLP11, BTAÖ13]. As for the aspect of partitioning and data transfer we want to evaluate the following three strategies:

1. Partitioning of both relations equally across all n_{join} nodes. This results in a constant amount of data to be transferred. This can be done with the Grace Join.
2. Replication of the smaller relation across all n_{join} nodes. This results in a data amount to be transferred which grows linearly with n_{join} nodes. After the completion of the data transfer, we want to execute the data item comparison which results in a minimal probing effort, at the price of a decreased degree of parallelism. This can be done with the distributed block-nested loop join (DBNLJ).

3. Replication of the smaller relation across all n_{join} nodes. This results in a data amount to be transferred which grows linearly with n_{join} nodes. During the data transfer, we want to execute the data item comparison which results in an increased probing effort, but enables data transfer and probing happening in parallel. This can be done with the Cyclo Join.

7.1 Grace Join

Grace Join algorithm: the Grace Join is described by Schneider and DeWitt [SD89] and is one of the standard join algorithms in the Gamma Database Machine Project [DGS+90]. The Grace Join can be divided into two phases as shown in Algorithm 1 and 2. The first phase partitions the data across all nodes $N_{1...i}^{join}$ used for executing the join. This happens by creating a number of buckets on each node $N_{1...i}^{part}$ that hold some data of a to-be-joined relation. The number of created buckets on each node matches the number of nodes that will be used for executing the join. The data from relation R and S on each node N_i^{part} is then hashed into the buckets. In a next step, those buckets are sent to the nodes executing the join. This hash partitioning of R and S across all nodes that execute the join ensures that all records which potentially match the join criteria are on the same node.

In the second phase (Algorithm 2), each node $N_{1...i}^{join}$ executes locally a simple hash join by hashing its data from S (which is considered to be smaller or equal than its data from R). A probing is then done against the resulting hash table by iterating over the data from R.

---

1 **foreach** $|R_i| / |S_i|$ **do**
2 $\quad\lfloor$ hash $|R_i| / |S_i|$ into $bucket_{i \bmod n_{join}}^{R/S}$;

3 **foreach** $bucket_i^{R/S}$ **do**
4 $\quad\lfloor$ send $bucket_i^{R/S}$ to host N_i^{join};

Algorithm 1: Grace Join partitioning phase at every $N_i^{part\,R/S}$

Grace Join system model: the Grace Join distributes the relations S and R over all nodes that participate in the join. This results in the transfer of both relations over the network minus the data of relations that does not have to be moved as the initial

---

1 **foreach** $|bucket_i^S|$ in $bucket_i^S$ **do**
2 $\quad\lfloor$ hash $|bucket_i^S|$ into $hashtable_S$;
3 **foreach** $|bucket_i^R|$ in $bucket_i^R$ **do**
4 $\quad\lfloor$ probe $|bucket_i^R|$ against $hashtable_S$;

Algorithm 2: Grace Join processing phase at every N_i^{join}

partitioning data placement equals the placement for join execution (Eq. 7.1). The total amount of bytes to be processed by hashing and probing (Eq. 7.4) consists of the initial hashing of the data for partitioning (Eqs. 7.5 and 7.6) and the hashing (Eq. 7.7) and probing (Eq. 7.8) of the partitioned data on each node for executing the simple hash-join. The total execution time (Eq. 7.9) is the sum of the time for partitioning the data and the join execution of each node. The time for hash-partitioning the data (Eqs. 7.10 and 7.11) is influenced by the initial partitioning of R and S and to what extent their data overlaps on nodes. The hashing of the data for partitioning and the transmission over the network to the join nodes (Eqs. 7.13–7.15) can be done in parallel. After the data distribution, the execution time is determined by executing the simple hash-join (Eq. 7.16). The partitioning phase and the join processing phase are modelled as non-overlapping as (a) the processing capabilities of the nodes can be fully utilized during the hash partitioning with the data being stored in memory and (b) to keep the number of probing operations constant during the join processing phase.

$$N_{tot} = N_r + N_s \tag{7.1}$$

$$N_r = R_{size} - \left(\frac{R_{size}}{n_{partR} * n_{join}} * \min(n_{partR}, n_{join}) \right) \tag{7.2}$$

$$N_s = S_{size} - \frac{n_{partOvl}}{n_{partS}} * \tag{7.3}$$

$$\left(\frac{S_{size}}{n_{partS} * n_{join}} * \min(n_{partS}, n_{join}) \right)$$

$$J_{tot} = J_{hashPartR} + J_{hashPartS} + J_{hash} + J_{probe} \tag{7.4}$$

$$J_{hashPartR} = R_{size} \tag{7.5}$$

$$J_{hashPartS} = S_{size} \tag{7.6}$$

$$J_{hash} = R_{size} \tag{7.7}$$

$$J_{probe} = S_{size} \tag{7.8}$$

$$T_{tot} = \max(T_{hashPart}, T_{net}) + T_{join} \tag{7.9}$$

$$T_{hashPart} = \max\left(\frac{J_{hashPartR}}{n_{partR} * BW_{hash}}, \frac{J_{hashPartS}}{n_{partS} * BW_{hash}} \right) \tag{7.10}$$

$$\text{if } n_{partOvl} = 0$$

$$= \frac{\frac{J_{hashPartR}}{n_{partR}} + \frac{J_{hashPartS}}{n_{partS}}}{BW_{hash}} \tag{7.11}$$

$$\text{if } n_{partOvl} > 0$$

$$T_{net} = \max(T_{send}, T_{recv}) \tag{7.12}$$

$$T_{send} = \max(\frac{N_r}{n_{partR} * BW_{net}}, \frac{N_s}{n_{partS} * BW_{net}}) \tag{7.13}$$

$$\text{if } n_{partOvl} = 0$$

$$= \frac{\frac{N_r}{n_{partR}} + \frac{N_s}{n_{partS}}}{BW_{net}} \tag{7.14}$$

$$\text{if } n_{partOvl} > 0$$

$$T_{recv} = \frac{N_s + N_r}{n_{join} * BW_{net}} \tag{7.15}$$

$$T_{join} = \frac{J_{hash}}{n_{join} * BW_{hash}} + \frac{J_{probe}}{n_{join} * BW_{probe}} \tag{7.16}$$

7.2 Distributed Block Nested Loop Join

Distributed Block Nested Loop Join algorithm: a Distributed Block Nested Loop Join performs a join between R and S by scanning every block of S tuples once for every block of R tuples. In a cluster, the data of R and S is distributed across a set of nodes and for processing the join, the blocks of R and S have to be exchanged between the respective nodes. The resulting network traffic can be reduced only by running the outer loop on each node by supplying each node $N_{1...i}^{join}$ with the entire relation S.

As depicted in Algorithm 3, each node N_i^{join} receives the complete relation S from $N_{1...i}^{part}$. If the number of nodes where the partitions S and R are partitioned across and the number of nodes used for join processing are not equal, then R also has to be distributed. However, each node N_i^{join} only receives a part of R where the size of the part depends on the number of nodes participating in the join. Once the data has been distributed, the join can be processed. Whether S or the respective part of R will be hashed or probed against, depends on their sizes.

Distributed Block Nested Loop Join system model: the DBNLJ—as specified in Algorithm 3—replicates the relation S on and distributes the relation R equally over every node that participates in the join. The resulting network transfer N_{tot} is the sum of both operations (Eq. 7.17). The network transfer for R is the distribution

---

1 **foreach** $N_{1...i}^{partR/S}$ **do**
2   **if** $n_{part} = n_{join}$ **then**
3 | receive S_i from N_i^{partS};
4   **else**
5 | receive $S_i, R_{i \mod n_{join}}$ from $N_i^{partR/S}$;

6 compute $R_i \bowtie S_i$ in memory;

Algorithm 3: BNLJ algorithm for every N_i^{join}

of R over all nodes that participates in the join (Eq. 7.18). The network transfer for S is the replication of parts of the relation to nodes that already hold some data of S and the full replication to extra nodes which might be added to the join execution (Eqs. 7.19 and 7.20). The total amount of bytes to be processed in memory for the join execution (Eq. 7.21) is the sum of hashing and probing. Since S is being replicated to all nodes, but each node only holds a part of R, it might be cheaper to hash R and probe over S (Eqs. 7.22–7.25). The total execution time (Eq. 7.26) is the sum of the time needed for partitioning the data (Eq. 7.27) as well as hashing and probing the data (Eq. 7.31). The time needed for partitioning the data across the nodes is determined by sending and receiving the data over the network (Eqs. 7.28–7.30).

$$N_{tot} = N_s + N_r \tag{7.17}$$

$$N_r = \frac{R_{size}}{n_{partR}} * \max(n_{partR} - n_{join}, 0) + \tag{7.18}$$

$$\frac{R_{size}}{n_{join}} * \max(n_{join} - n_{partR}, 0)$$

$$N_s = S_{size} * (n_{join} - 1) \tag{7.19}$$

$$\text{if } n_{join} \geq (n_{partR} + n_{partS} - n_{partOvl})$$

$$= S_{size} * (n_{join} - \frac{n_{join}}{n_{partR} + n_{partS} - n_{partOvl}}) \tag{7.20}$$

$$\text{if } n_{join} < (n_{partR} + n_{partS} - n_{partOvl})$$

$$J_{tot} = J_{hash} + J_{probe} \tag{7.21}$$

$$J_{hash} = S_{size} * n_{join} \qquad \text{if } \frac{R_{size}}{n_{join}} \geq S_{size} \tag{7.22}$$

$$= R_{size} \qquad \text{if } \frac{R_{size}}{n_{join}} < S_{size} \tag{7.23}$$

$$J_{probe} = R_{size} \qquad \text{if } \frac{R_{size}}{n_{join}} \geq S_{size} \tag{7.24}$$

$$= S_{size} * n_{join} \qquad \text{if } \frac{R_{size}}{n_{join}} < S_{size} \tag{7.25}$$

$$T_{tot} = T_{part} + T_{join} \tag{7.26}$$

$$T_{part} = \max(T_{send}, T_{recv}) \tag{7.27}$$

$$T_{send} = \max(\frac{N_r}{n_{partR} * BW_{net}}, \frac{N_s}{n_{partS} * BW_{net}}) \tag{7.28}$$

$$\text{if } n_{partOvl} = 0$$

$$= \frac{\frac{N_r}{n_{partR}} + \frac{N_s}{n_{partS}}}{BW_{net}} \tag{7.29}$$

$$\text{if } n_{partOvl} > 0$$

$$T_{recv} = \frac{N_s + N_r}{n_{join} * BW_{net}} \tag{7.30}$$

$$T_{join} = \frac{J_{hash}}{n_{join} * BW_{hash}} + \frac{J_{probe}}{n_{join} * BW_{probe}} \tag{7.31}$$

7.3 Cyclo Join

Cyclo Join algorithm: Frey, Goncalves, Kersten, and Teubner introduced the Cyclo Join [FGKT10] as a way to exploit inter-node bandwidth for join processing by creating a virtual ring between the nodes that participate in the processing of a join. During the join processing, data is continuously being pumped through that ring, thereby allowing for a greater degree of parallelism. In order to minimize the impact of the network processing overhead and to utilize the in-memory data storage performance characteristics at the same time, RDMA is chosen as network technology of choice for Cyclo Join. Goncalves and Kersten describe the Data Cyclotron [GK11] as a complete ring-centered data processing architecture.

Algorithm 4 describes the Cyclo Join, where the algorithm is similar to the Distributed BNLJ algorithm as introduced in the previous subsection, except for the distribution of S. Before the join execution starts, relation R is equally distributed across all nodes $N_{1...i}^{join}$. Then each node N_i^{join} can in parallel calculate the join between $R_i \bowtie S_i$ and ship parts of S to the next node in the virtual ring. Whether S or R will be hashed or probed against, depends on their sizes as well as on n_{join}. After completion of the Cyclo Join, relation S has traversed in its entirety each node N_i^{join}.

---

1 **if** $n_{part} \neq n_{join}$ **then**
2   receive R_i mod n_{join} from N_i^{partR}
3 **foreach** *block* S_i *received from* $N_{(i-1)}^{join}$ mod n_{join} **do**
4   compute $R_i \bowtie S_i$ in memory;
5   forward S_i to host $N_{(i+1)}$ mod n_{join};

Algorithm 4: Cyclo Join algorithm for every N_i^{join}

Cyclo Join system model: the total network transfer (Eq. 7.32) for a Cyclo Join execution consists of the data transfer before the join execution and the cyclic data transfer during the join. Before the join execution, S and R are equally distributed across all nodes that participate in the join processing (Eqs. 7.33–7.35). During the join execution, S is fully replicated to every node via the virtual network ring (Eq. 7.36). The total amount of bytes to be processed in memory for the join execution (Eq. 7.37) is the sum of hashing and probing. Since the number of probing operations grows with the number of nodes participating in the join, either the hashing or the probing operations can dominate the join execution. Therefore, two helper equations (Eqs. 7.38 and 7.39) are being introduced to determine if the total execution time of the join processing is smaller if S or R are being hashed or probed against. Equations (Eqs. 7.40–7.43) use these functions and provide the resulting amount of bytes to be processed in-memory for hashing and probing. The total execution time for a Cyclo Join (Eq. 7.44) consists of the initial data partitioning as well as the cyclic data transfer and the join processing. The time for the initial data partitioning (Eq. 7.45) includes the time for distributing S and R equally (Eqs. 7.46–7.48) and for hashing either S or R. Since the cyclic data transfer of S and the probing can happen in parallel, T_{cyc} (Eq. 7.49) is dominated by the more time-consuming operation of the two.

$$N_{tot} = N_{partR} + N_{partS} + N_{cyc} \tag{7.32}$$

$$N_{partR} = \frac{R_{size}}{n_{partR}} * \max(n_{partR} - n_{join}, 0) + \tag{7.33}$$

$$\frac{R_{size}}{n_{join}} * \max(n_{join} - n_{partR}, 0)$$

$$N_{partS} = \frac{S_{size}}{n_{join}} * max(n_{partS} - n_{join}, 0) \tag{7.34}$$

$$\text{if } n_{join} \geq (n_{partR} + n_{partS} - n_{partOvl})$$

$$= S_{size} - \frac{S_{size}}{n_{partS}} * max(n_{partR} - n_{join}, 0) \tag{7.35}$$

$$\text{if } n_{join} < (n_{partR} + n_{partS} - n_{partOvl})$$

$$N_{Cyc} = (n_{join} - 1) * S_{size} \tag{7.36}$$

$$J_{tot} = J_{hash} + J_{probe} \tag{7.37}$$

$$T^s_{hash} = \frac{S_{size}}{BW_{hash}} + \frac{R_{size} * n_{join}}{BW_{probe}} \tag{7.38}$$

$$T^r_{hash} = \frac{R_{size}}{BW_{hash}} + \frac{S_{size} * n_{join}}{BW_{probe}} \tag{7.39}$$

$$J_{hash} = S_{size} \qquad \text{if } T^s_{hash} < T^r_{hash} \tag{7.40}$$

$$= R_{size} \qquad \text{if } T^s_{hash} \geq T^r_{hash} \tag{7.41}$$

$$J_{probe} = R_{size} * n_{join} \qquad \text{if } T^s_{hash} < T^r_{hash} \tag{7.42}$$

$$= S_{size} * n_{join} \qquad \text{if } T^s_{hash} \geq T^r_{hash} \tag{7.43}$$

$$T_{tot} = T_{part} + T_{cyc} \tag{7.44}$$

$$T_{part} = \max(T_{send}, T_{recv}) + \frac{J_{hash}}{BW_{hash} * n_{join}} \tag{7.45}$$

$$T_{send} = \max(\frac{N_{partR}}{n_{partR} * BW_{net}}, \frac{N_{partS}}{n_{partS} * BW_{net}}) \tag{7.46}$$

$$\text{if } n_{partOvl} = 0$$

$$= \frac{\frac{N_{partR}}{n_{partR}} + \frac{N_{partS}}{n_{partS}}}{BW_{net}} \tag{7.47}$$

$$\text{if } n_{partOvl} > 0$$

$$T_{recv} = \frac{N_{partS} + N_{partR}}{n_{join} * BW_{net}} \tag{7.48}$$

$$T_{cyc} = \max(\frac{N_{cyc}}{BW_{net} * n_{join}}, \frac{J_{probe}}{BW_{probe} * n_{join}}) \tag{7.49}$$

7.4 Join Algorithm Comparison

We implemented the system model from the previous section in the statistical language R and prototypically implemented the join algorithms in RAMCloud in order to compare the different algorithms. Figure 7.1 illustrates a set of comparisons based on the parameters shown in Table 7.2. The comparisons reveal the execution times of a single join operation in a RAMCloud cluster with 16 nodes. Figure 7.1a, c are calculations based on the system model, Fig. 7.1b, d are the respective experimental validations based on the prototypical implementations. The size of relation S is changed between the first and the second calculation and validation.

Figure 7.1a, b indicate that the Grace Join is preferable when joining evenly sized relations. At n_{join} = 16 nodes, the Grace Join produces an N_{tot} of 1.8 GB where the DBNLJ and the Cyclo Join each transfer 15 GB over the network for executing the join due to their replication of the complete relation S to all nodes. This also spikes the amount of data to be processed (e.g. J_{tot} Grace Join = 4 GB vs. Cyclo Join = 17 GB) as the full relation S is traversed at every node (as shown in Fig. 7.2). Figure 7.1c, d show that the Cyclo Join performs best when one relation is substantially smaller than the other one. In addition, a small relation S lets the Cyclo Join benefit from its high degree of parallelism without introducing a noteworthy penalty for the additional probing (as shown in Fig. 7.2c, d). Concluding the comparison, the Grace Join and the Cyclo Join are the winners in the context of our chosen execution strategies when one join is executed at a time. We observe that choosing the right algorithm is heavily influenced by the sizes of the joined relations.

With regards to the validation of the system model, we observe that the measurements are about 20–25 % off in comparison to the system model. The reasons for

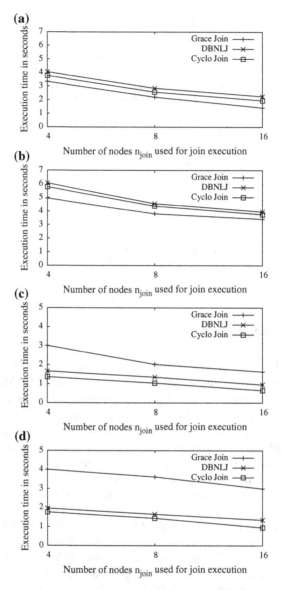

Fig. 7.1 Four comparisons of the execution times for different join algorithms. Figure 7.1a, c are calculations based on the system model, Fig. 7.1b, d are the respective experiments based on the prototypical implementations. **a** Calculation with system model for: $n_{partR/S} = 16$ nodes, $n_{partOvl} = 16$ nodes, $R_{size} = 1$ GB, $S_{size} = 1$ GB, **b** Experiment with implementation: $n_{partR/S} = 16$ nodes, $n_{partOvl} = 16$ nodes, $R_{size} = 1$ GB, $S_{size} = 1$ GB, **c** Calculation with system model for: $n_{partR/S} = 16$ nodes, $n_{partOvl} = 16$ nodes, $R_{size} = 1$ GB, $S_{size} = 0.1$ GB, **d** Experiment with implementation: $n_{partR/S} = 16$ nodes, $n_{partOvl} = 16$ nodes, $R_{size} = 1$ GB, $S_{size} = 0.1$ GB

Table 7.2 Hardware parameters

Parameter	Value
CPU	Intel Xeon X3470 CPU
NIC	Mellanox ConnectX-2 InfiniBand HCA
BW_{net}	3.142 GB/sec network bandwidth two nodes
BW_{hash}	0.107 GB/sec throughput for inserting into std::unordered_set
BW_{probe}	0.731 GB/sec throughput for probing against std::unordered_set

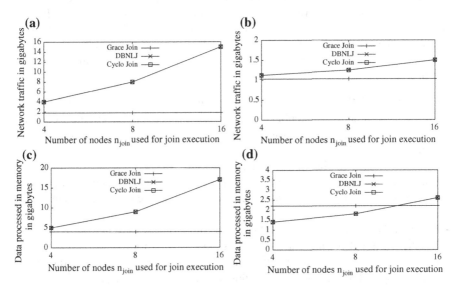

Fig. 7.2 Four comparisons of the network transfer and data processed in memory for different join algorithms. Figure 7.2**a**+**b** depict the network transfer N_{tot}, Fig. 7.2**c**+**d** illustrate the data amount processed in memory J_{tot}. **a** N_{tot} based on the system model for: $n_{partR/S} = 16$ nodes, $n_{partOvl} = 16$ nodes, $R_{size} = 1$ GB, $S_{size} = 1$ GB, **b** N_{tot} based on the system model for: $n_{partR/S} = 16$ nodes, $n_{partOvl} = 16$ nodes, $R_{size} = 1$ GB, $S_{size} = 0.1$ GB, **c** J_{tot} based on the system model for: $n_{partR/S} = 16$ nodes, $n_{partOvl} = 16$ nodes, $R_{size} = 1$ GB, $S_{size} = 1$ GB, **d** J_{tot} based on the system model for: $n_{partR/S} = 16$ nodes, $n_{partOvl} = 16$ nodes, $R_{size} = 1$ GB, $S_{size} = 0.1$ GB

that are, on the one hand, that our system model abstracts from resource conflicts and assumes a perfect distribution of network bandwidth among clients. On the other hand, our implementation in RAMCloud is not fully optimized, as we currently are working with dynamically growing data structures instead of estimating the data structure size and preallocating memory accordingly.

7.5 Parallel Join Executions

After comparing the execution of one join operation at a time, we now address the execution of many join operations in parallel via a simulation based on the previously created R-model. We take the join operations from the Star Schema Benchmark [O'N] at a sizing factor 100 (which has 600 million records in its main table) as workload as they vary in to-be-joined relations, relation sizes, and selectivity (as shown in the Tables 11.1 and 11.2 in the Appendix). Our goal is to execute this workload as fast as possible. The execution of the join operations in the workload happens sequentially (no change in the execution order), although join operations from different queries can run in parallel. Furthermore, we execute one join operation per RAMCloud node at a time. We introduce a set of heuristics that can decide at run-time how to parameterize the execution of a join operation. These parameters include the number of nodes to be used for executing the join (n_{join}) and the choice of the algorithm. The heuristics are:

- **Greedy Heuristic.** The Greedy Heuristic uses all nodes in the cluster for every join. This results in a sequential execution of all join operations in the workload. For each join operation the fastest algorithm is determined via the system model (with $n_{join} = n$).
- **Modest Heuristic.** This heuristic uses one-fourth of the nodes in the cluster for every join. This results in up to four join executions being executed in parallel. For each join operation the fastest algorithm is determined via the system model (with $n_{join} = \frac{n}{4}$).
- **Graceful Heuristic.** The Graceful Heuristic monitors the current load of the cluster and takes half of the currently idling nodes (where idling is defined as not currently executing a join) for the join execution. For each join operation the optimal algorithm is determined via the system model (with $n_{join} = \frac{\text{idling } n}{2}$).
- **Smart Heuristic.** This heuristic calculates for every join the to-be-used number of nodes and algorithm with the most efficient hardware utilization based on the cost model (minimal $\frac{T_{tot}}{n_{join}}$).

In addition to the above heuristics we also introduce a set of different partitioning strategies:

- **All Relations Uniform.** All relations are uniformly partitioned across all nodes.
- **All Relations Round-Robin.** All relations are distributed in a round-robin manner over four nodes at a time.
- **Small Relations Pinned - Large Relations Uniform.** Small relations are pinned on one node, large relations are partitioned uniformly across the remaining nodes.

Figure 7.3 illustrates the resulting execution times, showing that the partitioning of the large relations across all nodes in the cluster is preferable over placing them on only a few nodes each. The choice of the partitioning criteria has potentially more impact than the choice of the heuristic. When comparing the heuristics, one can see that the Modest Heuristic always performs best while the Smart and the Graceful

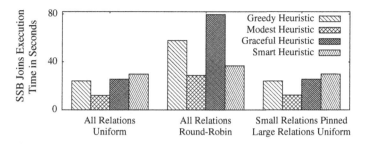

Fig. 7.3 Evaluation of join execution heuristics on a cluster with 32 nodes and hardware parameters shown in Table 7.2

Table 7.3 Distribution of join algorithms for Star Schema Benchmark execution as shown in Fig. 7.3 in dependence of the chosen heuristic

	All Relations Uniform			All Relations Round-Robin			Small Pinned, Large Uniform		
	Grace	DBNLJ	Cyclo	Grace	DBNLJ	Cyclo	Grace	DBNLJ	Cyclo
Greedy	36	0	0	36	0	0	19	0	17
Modest	30	0	6	11	0	25	30	0	6
Graceful	36	0	0	36	0	0	36	0	0
Smart	32	0	4	17	0	19	34	0	2

Illustration how many of the 36 joins are executed with which algorithm

Heuristics perform worse. This is due to executing each join very efficiently, but resulting in an overall bad cluster utilization. When looking at the chosen algorithms, Table 7.3 reports that the Grace Join and the Cyclo Join were chosen exclusively. Depending on the heuristic, either only the Grace Join has been used or in conjunction with the Cyclo Join. The winning Modest Heuristic always picked a mix of the Grace Join and the Cyclo Join. Concluding this section, the evaluation shows that (a) it is preferable to partition the data across as many nodes as possible and (b) perform the join operations with a mix of the Grace and the Cyclo Join. Furthermore, it is preferable to allocate a fixed number of nodes for the execution of each join as choosing the number of nodes based on efficient join execution or cluster load leads to under utilization of the cluster.

Part III
Evaluation

Chapter 8
Performance Evaluation

This chapter presents a performance evaluation to quantify the gap between query execution on local and remote main memory while considering the different operator execution strategies (data pull vs. operator push). Two different workloads are being used: an analytical workload consisting of the Star Schema Benchmark in Sect. 8.1 and a mixed workload based on point-of-sales customer data from a large European retailer in Sect. 8.2. The used hardware is the same as in the previous part. Each node has an Intel Xeon X3470 CPU, 24GB DDR3 DRAM, and a Mellanox ConnectX-2 InfiniBand HCA network interface card with the nodes connected via a 36-port Mellanox InfiniScale IV (4X QDR) switch.

8.1 Analytical Workload: Star Schema Benchmark

Figure 8.1 shows an AnalyticsDB operator breakdown for each query of the Star Schema Benchmark (SSB). AnalyticsDB runs on a single node, the RAMCloud cluster has 20 nodes. The execution on RAMCloud happens either via data pull or operator push strategy and each AnalyticsDB column is either being stored on one storage node (server span=1) or partitioned across all nodes (server span=20). The figure illustrates that the partitioning criteria has only very little impact (2.8 %) on the data pull execution strategy and that data pull is on average 2.6 times slower than the execution on local DRAM. With a server span of one, the operator push execution strategy is on average 11 % slower than the execution on local DRAM. With a server span of 20, the operator execution strategy can be accelerated by a factor of 3.4. The figure does not show the execution times of the local AnalyticsDB operators such as Sort in detail, but summarizes them as *Other Operators*.

Figure 8.2 evaluates the impact a varying data set size has on the execution time by showing the execution of the SSB with a varying data scale factor SF. Scale factor 1 has a fact table with 6 million rows and a total data size of 600 MB, scale factor 10 has a fact table with 60 million rows and a total data set size of 6 GB, and scale factor 100 has 600 million rows in the fact table and a total data set size of 60 GB.

© Springer International Publishing Switzerland 2016   95
C. Tinnefeld, *Building a Columnar Database on RAMCloud*, In-Memory
Data Management Research, DOI 10.1007/978-3-319-20711-7_8

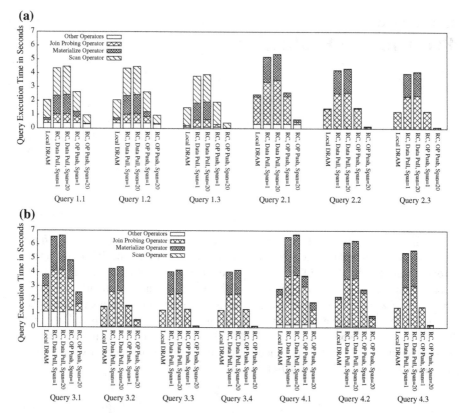

Fig. 8.1 Operator breakdown for AnalyticsDB executing Star Schema Benchmark queries with a data scale factor of 10 and different storage options and operator execution strategies. AnalyticsDB runs on a single node, the RAMCloud (RC) cluster has size of 20 nodes. The figure illustrates that the data pull execution strategy is on average 2.6 times (or 260 %) slower than the execution on local DRAM and that the operator push execution strategy is on average 11 % slower than the execution on local DRAM. **a** Star Schema Benchmark Queries 1.1–2.3. **b** Star Schema Benchmark Queries 3.1–4.3

The experiments with SF 100 could not be executed on local DRAM as the data set size exceeded the capacity of a single server. Figure 8.2 illustrates that the ratio between the data set size and the SSB execution times of the different execution strategies remain constant even with a growing data set size and with a constant cluster size.

Throughout the previous experiments, we varied the number of nodes in the RAM-Cloud cluster and the resulting server span. In this subsection, we want to perform this variation not in separate experiment executions, but continuously while a single AnalyticsDB node is executing queries. Therefore, we designed and used a simplistic data migration manager which distributes the data equally across the available nodes: if a new node joins the RAMCloud cluster, it gets a chunk of the data, before a node

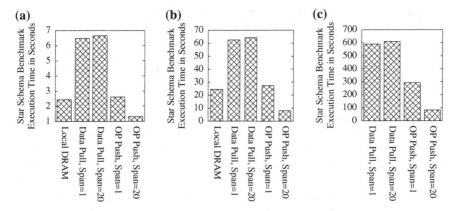

Fig. 8.2 RAMCloud cluster with 20 nodes and a single node running AnalyticsDB with a varying Star Schema Benchmark data scale factor (SF). The figure shows that the ratio between data set size and Star Schema Benchmark execution times remain constant with a growing data set size. **a** Sizing Factor = 1, **b** Sizing Factor = 10, **c** Sizing Factor = 100

is removed from the cluster its contained data is distributed across the remaining nodes. The data distribution is done via a splitting of the RAMCloud namespaces and a subsequent migration of the data that is contained in a part of a namespace: the complexity and execution time of this mechanism benefits from an equal partitioning of all namespaces.

Figure 8.3 illustrates the SSB execution time while RAMCloud nodes are being added or removed from the cluster. With every added RAMCloud node, the overall storage capacity increases and the SSB execution time decreases as previously discussed. With every removed node the overall storage capacity decreases and the SSB execution time increases.

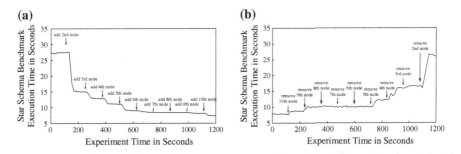

Fig. 8.3 RAMCloud cluster with a varying number of nodes and a single node running AnalyticsDB with a operator push execution strategy and a Star Schema Benchmark data scale factor of 10

8.2 Mixed Workload: Point-of-Sales Customer Data

This section also aims to quantify the gap between query execution on local and remote main memory while considering the different operator execution strategies (data pull vs. operator push). In contrast to the previous section, it is not done by taking a synthetic benchmark with generated data, but an excerpt of the point-of-sales data from one of the largest European retailers with over 5,000 branches. The excerpt includes about 62 million records, which is a data volume of 10.8 GB and holds the point-of-sales data of some branches over the course of a month. Each record represents a single product being sold at the cash register in a single branch. The point-of-sales data itself is in a single fact table accompanied by a number of dimension tables which describe the different branches and products. Products are hierarchically grouped in four levels where Product Group Level 1 contains for example all non-alcoholic drinks, Product Group Level 2 contains all soft drinks, Product Group Level 3 contains all energy drinks and Product Level 4 contains the different actual products where each variation of a product in size or flavor is a separate product.

The workload itself consists of four analytical and one transactional query. The analytical queries represent how a sales analyst operates on the data, while the transactional query covers a product being sold at a cash register. The following queries are used:

- AQ1: The first analytical query calculates the grouping of all sold items by Product Group Level 1, showing for example which percentage of the overall sales was achieved by non-alcoholic drinks.

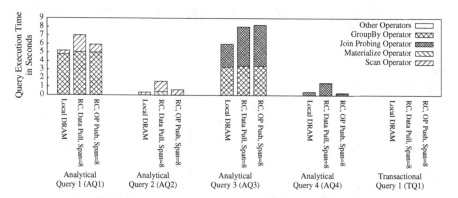

Fig. 8.4 Operator breakdown for executing the customer data mixed workload. Operator breakdown for executing the point-of-sales customer data mixed workload with different operator execution strategies. AnalyticsDB runs on a single node, the RAMCloud (RC) cluster has a size of 8 nodes. The figure illustrates i.a. that the data pull execution strategy is on average 2.2x slower than the execution on local DRAM and that the operator push execution strategy is on average 44 % slower than the execution on local DRAM

- AQ2: This analytical query lists how often a single product has been sold for what price, analyzing the price elasticity of a product.
- AQ3: This query groups all sales by a chosen Product Group Level 2 and shows the respective revenues and quantities. This query has a low selectivity as it groups by a product group that includes many sold products.
- AQ4: Same as AQ3 but with selecting a product group where only few products were sold resulting in a high selectivity.
- TQ1: This query performs an insert for a sold product that was registered at the counter.

Figure 8.4 presents the operator breakdown for executing the customer data mixed workload with different operator execution strategies. AnalyticsDB runs on a single node, the RAMCloud cluster has a size of 8 nodes. The outcome of the experiment is similar to the experiment presented in Sect. 8.1: for the queries AQ1–AQ4 the data pull execution strategy is on average 2.3x slower, the operator push execution strategy is on average 44 % slower. It can be observed that in query AQ3 the operator push execution strategy is slower than the data pull strategy due to the low selectivity, whereas in query AQ4 the operator push execution strategy is even faster than an execution on local DRAM due to parallelism in RAMCloud in combination with high selectivity. The transactional query takes 4 μs on local DRAM and 12 μs with RAMCloud regardless of the operator execution strategy.

Chapter 9
High-Availability Evaluation

As shown in Fig. 8.3 in the previous chapter, the size of a RAMCloud Cluster can be changed without an interruption of the query processing executed by AnalyticsDB. However, the dynamic resizing in Fig. 8.3b is done via a purposeful revocation of a node which gives RAMCloud the time to redistribute the data from the to-be-removed node before its actual revocation. This kind of awareness cannot be expected in the event of a hardware failure. For the scenario of an unexpected hardware failure, RAMCloud features a fast crash recovery mechanism [ORS$^+$11] as explained in Sect. 3.3.

AnalyticsDB can make use of the fast crash recovery feature in RAMCloud. To prove its applicability in the context of a database application, we conduct the following experiment: the experiment utilizes a total of 20 nodes where 10 nodes run the RAMCloud master service as well as the RAMCloud backup service. The number of replicas is set to three. The remaining 10 nodes run AnalyticsDB which consecutively executes the Star Schema Benchmark suite to create a base load on the cluster. The Star Schema Benchmark data set is sized at factor 10.

In this experiment, each AnalyticsDB node permanently executes the Star Schema Benchmark. At a sizing factor 10, the average runtime is about 8.2 s. As shown in Fig. 9.1, after about 60 s, one RAMCloud node is getting killed, decreasing the total RAMCloud node count to 9 running nodes within the cluster. When a RAMCloud node is killed, its data is restored from the backups to the remaining servers.

The RAMCloud data recovery process itself takes between 0.2 and 0.5 s. At a SSB sizing factor 10 the overall dataset is about 6 GB, resulting in about 600 MB of data per node at the initial setup of 10 RAMCloud nodes. It is possible that an AnalyticsDB node is connected to the RAMCloud node that is being killed and executes an operator. Here, the AnalyticsDB node is not notified in any way of the crashed RAMCloud node. For that case, AnalyticsDB has a RPC timeout of 1 s after which the respective RPC is issued again. This RPC timeout also explains the execution time bumps in Fig. 9.1 which are greater than just the time needed for the RAMCloud recovery process.

© Springer International Publishing Switzerland 2016

C. Tinnefeld, *Building a Columnar Database on RAMCloud*, In-Memory
Data Management Research, DOI 10.1007/978-3-319-20711-7_9

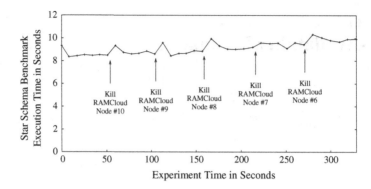

Fig. 9.1 High-availability experiment with one AnalyticsDB and ten RAMCloud nodes. Throughout the experiment RAMCloud nodes get killed and the impact on the query response time is observed

AnalyticsDB is not aware of the fact that a node of its storage system was killed, it just notices the timed-out RPC and restarts it. Throughout the experiment in Fig. 9.1, the execution time of the Star Schema Benchmark execution increases as the capacity of the RAMCloud cluster decreases constantly.

Chapter 10
Elasticity Evaluation

In the previous experiments in our evaluation, we varied either the number of RAM-Cloud nodes or we varied the load by changing the number of AnalyticsDB nodes. In this chapter we want to put the pieces together by maintaining a constant query execution time by resizing the RAMCloud cluster online under a changing load which is represented by a varying amount of AnalyticsDB nodes executing the Star Schema Benchmark.

The experiments in this chapter define an upper and lower execution time limit for the average Star Schema Benchmark execution time of 30 and 20 seconds respectively. If the load is increased by adding AnalyticsDB nodes and subsequently the execution time goes above the upper limit, then new RAMCloud nodes are added to the cluster until the average execution is back within the boundaries. The same approach is used when AnalyticsDB nodes are being removed and the execution time drops below the lower limit resulting in the removal of RAMCloud nodes. It is common to take differently shaped workloads for evaluating the elasticity of a system [ILFL12, CST$^+$10]: we use three different workloads namely a sinus-shaped, a plateau-shaped, and an exponential workload. We added a simplistic load manager to the system, as the RAMCloud project does not feature such a component as of now, which checks on configurable intervals the average processing time of the Star Schema Benchmark and adds or removes RAMCloud nodes accordingly.

Sinus-Shaped Workload

The first experiment we present executes a sinus-shaped workload. In the beginning, only one AnalyticsDB node executes the SSB benchmark, after a while a second node, then three more nodes and finally five nodes are added. The experiments highest load counts ten AnalyticsDB nodes in total. Following the sinus shape, after a while, five nodes, then three nodes and finally one node are removed to lower the load back to the initial load. Once the load manager detects a breach of the upper bound, it will check another 90 times before acting. The delay of the lower bound

© Springer International Publishing Switzerland 2016
C. Tinnefeld, *Building a Columnar Database on RAMCloud*, In-Memory
Data Management Research, DOI 10.1007/978-3-319-20711-7_10

is set to 30 s, while the delay for the upper bound breach is three times higher than for the lower bound. This can be useful to avoid provisioning resources in case of runaways. On the other hand, a shorter delay helps the load manager to provision new resources faster and therefore react more elastically. Figure 10.1 shows a sinus-shaped workload pattern in which RAMCloud scales out and later back in as load is decreasing. The delay between breaching the upper bound and starting the second RAMCloud node is obvious. Since the load manager is a simple reactive manager, it only starts one RAMCloud node at a time leading to a period of slow mitigation from the moment of high load at about 500 s from the experiment's beginning. At about 700 s, the SSB runtime is back in its normal boundaries. With lowering the load, the system reacts faster with de-provisioning of nodes.

Plateau-Shaped Workload

The second experiment is depicted in Fig. 10.2. The upper and lower boundary for the SSB runtime are set to the same value (30 s upper and 20 s lower) as in the first experiment. One RAMCloud node is started at the beginning of the experiment. The cluster load is ramped up by starting an AnalyticsDB node every 60 s. In this experiment, the load manager delays acting upon a boundary violation by 300 ms. Because of the instantaneous under-provisioning situation, the load manager starts seven more RAMCloud nodes to bring the SSB execution time into the specified boundaries. The time period the cluster runs on high load is called plateau time. In this experiment, it is 600 s long. At about 1100 s, the plateau time is over. The benchmark framework stops 9 out of 10 AnalyticsDB nodes, reducing the cluster load to one-tenth of the plateau load. This leads to an immense over-provisioning situation. The runtime of the SSB benchmark drops to under 10 s per SSB run. The load manager acts immediately by stopping 7 of the 8 running nodes to bring the runtime back into its boundaries. The SSB runtime runs within boundaries until the end of the experiment.

Exponential Workload

In the third experiment, we probe an exponential workload. As shown in Fig. 10.3 the experiment starts with one AnalyticsDB node. After the second node has been added, first two then four nodes are added with a delay of 120 s. It is clearly visible, that the system needs much more time to normalize the SSB runtime when four nodes are being added to the system. This has two reasons: first, the load manager only adds one node at a time. With a more efficient load manager, it could be possible to start more RAMCloud nodes the more the load has increased. This would bring the execution time within the specified boundaries more quickly, but also bears the risk of oversteering. Second, the higher the load in the system, the longer it takes

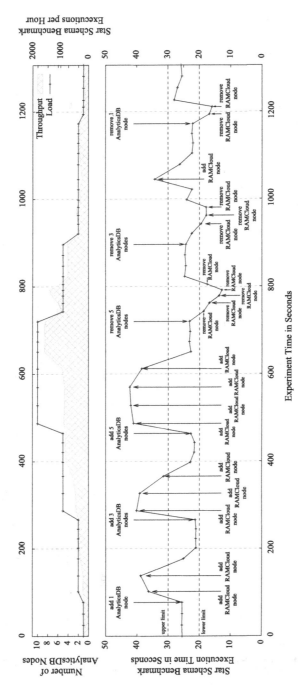

Fig. 10.1 Elasticity evaluation with a sinus-shaped workload. The number of the nodes in the RAMCloud cluster varies depending on the changing workload imposed by a changing number of AnalyticsDB nodes. Each AnalyticsDB node executes the Star Schema Benchmark at a sizing factor ten, the execution strategy is operator push

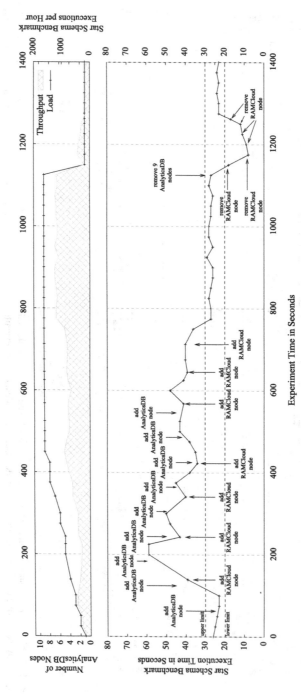

Fig. 10.2 Elasticity evaluation with a plateau-shaped workload. The number of the nodes in the RAMCloud cluster varies depending on the changing workload imposed by a changing number of AnalyticsDB nodes. Each AnalyticsDB node executes the Star Schema Benchmark at a sizing factor ten, the execution strategy is operator push

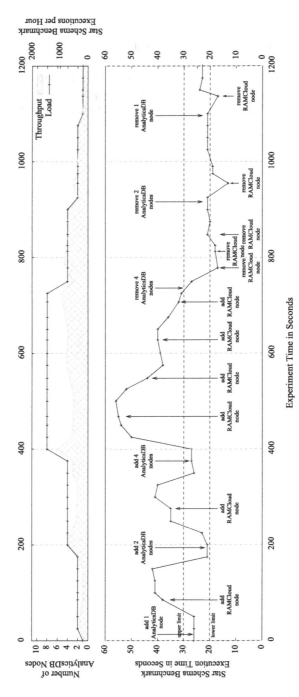

Fig. 10.3 Elasticity evaluation with an quadratically in- and decreasing workload. The number of the nodes in the RAMCloud cluster varies in dependence of a changing workload imposed by a changing number of AnalyticsDB nodes. Each AnalyticsDB node executes the Star Schema Benchmark at a sizing factor ten, the execution strategy is operator push

to migrate data between the nodes to distribute the load among more nodes. When the load decreases, the system corrects the over-provisioning situation by stopping RAMCloud nodes.

The experiments in this chapter (a) show that the architecture can adapt to workload changes of different orders in a short period of time (seconds), (b) the adaption does not interrupt the ongoing query processing and (c) the resulting elasticity allows the compliance with a performance goal without any adjustments from a DBMS perspective or without any manual intervention from a database administrator.

Part IV
Conclusions

Chapter 11
Conclusions

Current state-of-the-art parallel main memory DBMSs are designed according to the principles of a shared-nothing architecture driven by the intention of minimizing network traffic and thereby preserve the main memory performance advantage (as discussed in Chap. 2). The advent of RDMA-enabled network technology makes the creation of a parallel main memory DBMS based on a shared-storage technology feasible. A modern storage system such as RAMCloud keeps all data resident in main memory, provides durability, high-availability and is elastic: exploiting these characteristics in the context of a database management system is desirable. Nowadays, provisioning of information technology infrastructure over the Internet—including in-memory computing—allows the service providers to leverage the economies of scale and offer their services at an unbeatable price point. Being able to utilize hosted main memory-based storage for operating a database system makes in-memory data management even more economically viable.

Consequently, this work describes building a columnar database on shared main memory-based storage. The DBMS that is used throughout this work is AnalyticsDB which features dictionary-compression, a column-at-a-time execution model, applies the pattern of late materialization and is optimized for read-mostly respectively mixed workloads. Several instances of AnalyticsDB share a common access to main memory-based storage provided by RAMCloud, in combination with RDMA-enabled network.

Part I of this work describes that AnalyticsDB features an encapsulation of data access and operator execution via an interface which allows seamlessly switching between local or remote main memory. Since RAMCloud provides not only storage capacity but also processing power, this allows for pushing-down the execution of database operators into the storage system. Part I also shows that the data of a column-oriented DBMS can be persisted in a hash table while at the same time maintaining the fast scan speed when working on column-oriented data by chopping up a column into small blocks and storing each block as a key-value pair. We demonstrated that with a tuple size of 8-bytes a block size of 1000 tuples is sufficient to achieve the same scan speed as with a completely sequential placement of all tuples.

© Springer International Publishing Switzerland 2016

C. Tinnefeld, *Building a Columnar Database on RAMCloud*, In-Memory Data Management Research, DOI 10.1007/978-3-319-20711-7_11

Part II tackles the problem of placing the execution of database operators. The presented system model allows the estimation of operator execution costs in terms of network transfer, data processed in memory, and wall time. This can be used for database operators that work on one relation at a time—such as a scan or materialize operation—to discuss the site selection problem (data pull vs. operator push). Since a database query translates to the execution of several database operators, it is possible that the optimal site selection varies per operator. For the execution of a database operator that works on two (or more) relations at a time—such as a join—the system model is enriched by additional factors such as the chosen algorithm (e.g. Grace- vs. DBNL- vs. Cyclo-Join), the data partitioning of the respective relations and their overlapping as well as the allowed resource allocation.

Part III presents an evaluation of AnalyticsDB on RAMCloud on a cluster with 60 nodes where all nodes are connected via RDMA-enabled network equipment. We show that query processing performance is about 2.4x slower if everything is done via the data pull operator execution strategy (i.e. RAMCloud is being used only for data access), and about 27% slower if operator execution is also supported inside RAMCloud (in comparison to operating only on main memory inside a server without any network communication). The fast-crash recovery feature of RAMCloud can be leveraged for providing high-availability (e.g. a server crash during query execution only delays the query response for about one second). Our solution is elastic in a way that it adapts to changing workloads (a) within seconds (b) without interruption of the ongoing query processing and (c) without manual intervention.

A closing remark: this work comes to the conclusion that deploying a parallel main memory-based DBMS on a storage system such as RAMCloud allows leveraging the features of the storage system, but incorporates a performance penalty in comparison to operating on local main memory. Is this a beneficial trade-off? We believe *yes*: (a) When operating a system at scale, the scalability and elasticity of the overall system is more important than the last percentage points of performance. (b) This approach enables the main memory DBMS to neglect the aspect of data durability— which currently is a complex aspect of a main memory DBMS. (c) The comparison to operating on local main memory for quantifying the performance penalties references the best-case scenario which is not achievable in any parallel DBMS architecture.

Appendix

See Tables A.1 and A.2.

Table A.1 Star Schema Benchmark relations involved in joins operations. One record has a size of 8 bytes

Relation name	ID	Number of records in SF1
LineOrder::Custkey	R1	6,000,000
LineOrder::Orderdate	R2	6,000,000
LineOrder:Partkey	R3	6,000,000
LineOrder::Suppkey	R4	6,000,000
Customer::Custkey	S1	150,000
Date::Datekey	S2	2556
Part::Partkey	S3	200,000
Supplier::Suppkey	S4	10,000

© Springer International Publishing Switzerland 2016
C. Tinnefeld, *Building a Columnar Database on RAMCloud*, In-Memory
Data Management Research, DOI 10.1007/978-3-319-20711-7

Table A.2 Star Schema Benchmark join operations

Join ID	Query ID	R ID	R Selectivity	S ID	S Selectivity
J1	Query 1.1	R2	0.136	S2	0.142
J2	Query 1.2	R2	0.054	S2	0.011
J3	Query 1.3	R2	0.027	S2	0.002
J4	Query 2.1	R3	1	S3	0.04
J5	Query 2.1	R4	0.04	S4	0.2
J6	Query 2.1	R2	0.008	S2	1
J7	Query 2.2	R3	1	S3	0.008
J8	Query 2.2	R4	0.008	S4	0.2
J9	Query 2.2	R2	0.0016	S2	1
J10	Query 2.3	R3	1	S3	0.001
J11	Query 2.3	R4	0.001	S4	0.2
J12	Query 2.3	R2	0.0002	S2	1
J13	Query 3.1	R1	1	S1	0.2
J14	Query 3.1	R4	0.2	S4	0.2
J15	Query 3.1	R2	0.04	S2	1
J16	Query 3.2	R1	1	S1	0.04
J17	Query 3.2	R4	0.04	S4	0.04
J18	Query 3.2	R2	0.0016	S2	0.86
J19	Query 3.3	R1	1	S1	0.008
J20	Query 3.3	R4	0.008	S4	0.008
J21	Query 3.3	R2	0.00006	S2	0.86
J22	Query 3.4	R1	1	S1	0.008
J23	Query 3.4	R4	0.008	S4	0.008
J24	Query 3.4	R2	0.00006	S2	0.012
J25	Query 4.1	R1	1	S1	0.2
J26	Query 4.1	R4	0.2	S4	0.2
J27	Query 4.1	R3	0.04	S3	0.4
J28	Query 4.1	R2	0.016	S2	1
J29	Query 4.2	R1	1	S1	0.2
J30	Query 4.2	R4	0.2	S4	0.2
J31	Query 4.2	R3	0.04	S3	0.4
J32	Query 4.2	R2	0.016	S2	0.285
J33	Query 4.3	R3	1	S3	0.008
J34	Query 4.3	R4	0.08	S4	0.04
J35	Query 4.3	R1	0.00003	S1	0.2
J36	Query 4.3	R2	0.00006	S2	0.285

Glossary

AnalyticsDB is a prototypical in-memory DBMS written in C++ that can seamlessly switch between local and remote main memory.

CPU Central Processing Unit.

Cloud Computing is a paradigm that describes the provisioning of information technology infrastructure, services, and applications over the Internet.

Cloud Storage System manages and persists large amounts of data created and consumed by cloud computing applications.

Column-Oriented Data Layout stores all the instances of the same attribute type from different tuples physically together.

Database is a collection of related data [EN10].

Database Management System (DBMS) is a collection of programs that enables users to create and maintain a database. The DBMS is a general purpose software system that facilitates the processes of defining, constructing, manipulating, and sharing databases among various users and applications [EN10].

Database Operator evaluates a condition on a set of tuples.

Database-Aware Storage System directly executes database operators inside the storage system [RGF98, Kee99, SBADAD05]. This approach is based on the idea of active storage/active disks/intelligent disks where the computational power inside the storage device is being used for moving computation closer to the data [AUS98, KPH98].

DBMS Database Management System.

Distributed Database is a collection of multiple, logically interrelated databases distributed over a computer network. A distributed database management system (DBMS) is then defined as the software system that permits the management of the distributed database system and makes the distribution transparent to the users [ÖV11].

Distributed Filesystem allows users of physically distributed computers to share data and storage resources by using a common file system [LS90].

DRAM Dynamic Random-Access Memory.

Elasticity is the ability to deal with load variations by adding more resources during high load or consolidating the tenants to fewer nodes when the load decreases,

© Springer International Publishing Switzerland 2016

C. Tinnefeld, *Building a Columnar Database on RAMCloud*, In-Memory Data Management Research, DOI 10.1007/978-3-319-20711-7

all in a live system without service disruption, and is therefore critical for these systems. Elasticity is critical to minimize operating costs while ensuring good performance during high loads. It allows consolidation of the system to consume less resources and thus minimize the operating cost during periods of low load while allowing it to dynamically scale up its size as the load decreases [AEADE11].

ETL   Extract, Transform, and Load.

InfiniBand   is a switched fabric computer network communications link.

IMDB   In-Memory Database.

In-Memory Database (IMDB)   system, also referred to as main memory database system, is a database system where data resides permanently in main physical memory [GMS92].

Mixed Workload   is a database workload that includes transactional as well as analytical queries [Pla09].

MMDB   Main Memory Database, see In-Memory Database.

NoSQL   is most commonly referred to as "not only SQL". This term does not reject the query language SQL, but rather expresses that the design of relational database management systems is unsuitable for large-scale cloud applications [Bur10].

OLAP   Online Analytical Processing.

OLTP   Online Transaction Processing.

Parallel Database Management System (DBMS)   is a revision and extension of a distributed database management system that exploits the parallel nature of an underlying computing system in order to accelerate query execution [DG92].

RAMCloud   is a storage system from Stanford University where data is kept entirely in DRAM [OAE+11].

RDMA   Remote Direct Memory Access.

Remote Direct Memory Access (RDMA)   Remote Direct Memory Access enables the network interface card to transfer data directly into the main memory, bypassing the operating system by eliminating the need to copy data into the data buffers in the operating system (which is also known as zero-copy networking). In addition, transferring data via RDMA can be done without invoking the CPU [Mel13].

Row-Oriented Data Layout   stores all attributes of a tuple physically together.

Scalability   is a desirable property of a system, which indicates its ability to either handle growing amounts of work in a graceful manner or its ability to improve throughput when additional resources (typically hardware) are added. A system whose performance improves after adding hardware, proportionally to the capacity added, is said to be a scalable system [AEADE11].

Shared-memory   (or shared-everything) is an architectural approach for a parallel database management system where all processors share direct access to any main memory module and to all disks over an interconnection [ÖV11].

Shared-storage   (or shared-disk or shared-data) is an architectural approach for a parallel database management system where processors each have their own memory, but they share access to a single collection of storage devices such as a hard-disk [ÖV11].

Shared-storage   is an architectural approach for a parallel database management system where each memory and disk is owned by some processor which acts as a server for that data [ÖV11].

Site Selection   in the context of client-server computing, describes the decision whether to execute a query at the client machine at which the query was initiated or at the server machines that store the relevant data. In other words, the question is whether to move the query to the data (execution at servers) or to move the data to the query (execution at clients) [Kos00].

SSB   Star Schema Benchmark.

Star Schema Benchmark (SSB)   is an analytical database benchmark [O'N].

SQL   Structured (English) Query Language [CB74].

Switch Fabric Communication   describes a network topology where (a) each network node connects with each other via one or more switches, (b) the connection between two nodes is established based on the crossbar switch theory [Mat01] resulting in no resource conflicts with connections between any other nodes at the same time [GS02].

References

[ACC+10]   Daniel J. Abadi, Michael Carey, Surajit Chaudhuri, Hector Garcia-Molina, Jig-
            nesh M. Patel, and Raghu Ramakrishnan. let's. *Proc. VLDB Endow.*, 3(1-2):1657–
            1657, September 2010.
[ADHW99]   Anastassia Ailamaki, David J. DeWitt, Mark D. Hill, and David A. Wood. Dbmss
            on a modern processor: Where does time go? In Malcolm P. Atkinson, Maria E.
            Orlowska, Patrick Valduriez, Stanley B. Zdonik, and Michael L. Brodie, editors,
            *VLDB'99, Proceedings of 25th International Conference on Very Large Data Bases,
            September 7-10, 1999, Edinburgh, Scotland, UK*, pages 266–277. Morgan Kauf-
            mann, 1999.
[AEADE11]   Divyakant Agrawal, Amr El Abbadi, Sudipto Das, and Aaron J. Elmore. Database
            scalability, elasticity, and autonomy in the cloud. In *Proceedings of the 16th Inter-
            national Conference on Database Systems for Advanced Applications - Volume Part
            I*, DASFAA'11, pages 2–15, Berlin, Heidelberg, 2011. Springer-Verlag.
[AHK85]   Arthur C. Ammann, Maria Hanrahan, and Ravi Krishnamurthy. Design of a memory
            resident dbms. In *COMPCON*, pages 54–58. IEEE Computer Society, 1985.
[Amd67]   Gene M. Amdahl. Validity of the single processor approach to achieving large scale
            computing capabilities. In *Proceedings of the April 18-20, 1967, spring joint com-
            puter conference*, AFIPS '67 (Spring), pages 483–485, New York, NY, USA, 1967.
            ACM.
[AMD13]   AMD - Global Provider of Innovative Graphics, Processors and Media Solutions.
            http://www.amd.com, Last checked on July 23rd 2013.
[AMDM07]   Daniel J. Abadi, Daniel S. Myers, David J. DeWitt, and Samuel Madden. Mate-
            rialization Strategies in a Column-Oriented DBMS. In *Proceedings of the 23rd
            International Conference on Data Engineering, ICDE 2007, The Marmara Hotel,
            Istanbul, Turkey, April 15-20, 2007*, pages 466–475. IEEE, 2007.
[AMF06]   Daniel Abadi, Samuel Madden, and Miguel Ferreira. Integrating compression and
            execution in column-oriented database systems. In *Proceedings of the 2006 ACM
            SIGMOD international conference on Management of data*, SIGMOD '06, pages
            671–682, New York, NY, USA, 2006. ACM.
[AMH08]   Daniel J. Abadi, Samuel R. Madden, and Nabil Hachem. Column-stores vs. row-
            stores: how different are they really? In *Proceedings of the 2008 ACM SIGMOD
            international conference on Management of data*, SIGMOD '08, pages 967–980,
            New York, NY, USA, 2008. ACM.
[Ass13]   InfiniBand Trade Association. The infiniband architecture. http://www.infinibandta.
            org/content/pages.php?pg=technology_download, Last checked on July 23rd 2013.

© Springer International Publishing Switzerland 2016   119
C. Tinnefeld, *Building a Columnar Database on RAMCloud*, In-Memory
Data Management Research, DOI 10.1007/978-3-319-20711-7

[AUS98]   Anurag Acharya, Mustafa Uysal, and Joel Saltz. Active disks: programming model, algorithms and evaluation. In *Proceedings of the eighth international conference on Architectural support for programming languages and operating systems*, ASPLOS VIII, pages 81–91, New York, NY, USA, 1998. ACM.

[BCV91]   Björn Bergsten, Michel Couprie, and Patrick Valduriez. Prototyping dbs3, a shared-memory parallel database system. In *Proceedings of the First International Conference on Parallel and Distributed Information Systems (PDIS 1991)*, pages 226–234, 1991.

[BEH+10]   Dominic Battré, Stephan Ewen, Fabian Hueske, Odej Kao, Volker Markl, and Daniel Warneke. Nephele/pacts: A programming model and execution framework for web-scale analytical processing. In *Proceedings of the 1st ACM Symposium on Cloud Computing*, SoCC '10, pages 119–130, New York, NY, USA, 2010. ACM.

[BFG+08]   Matthias Brantner, Daniela Florescu, David A. Graf, Donald Kossmann, and Tim Kraska. Building a database on S3. In *Proceedings of the ACM SIGMOD International Conference on Management of Data, SIGMOD 2008, Vancouver, BC, Canada, June 10-12, 2008*, pages 251–264. ACM, 2008.

[BGK96]   Doug Burger, James R. Goodman, and Alain Kägi. Memory bandwidth limitations of future microprocessors. In *Proceedings of the 23rd annual international symposium on Computer architecture*, ISCA '96, pages 78–89, New York, NY, USA, 1996. ACM.

[BGvK+06]   Peter Boncz, Torsten Grust, Maurice van Keulen, Stefan Manegold, Jan Rittinger, and Jens Teubner. Monetdb/xquery: a fast xquery processor powered by a relational engine. In *Proceedings of the 2006 ACM SIGMOD international conference on Management of data*, SIGMOD '06, pages 479–490, New York, NY, USA, 2006. ACM.

[BKM08a]   Peter A. Boncz, Martin L. Kersten, and Stefan Manegold. Breaking the memory wall in monetdb. *Commun. ACM*, 51(12):77–85, December 2008.

[BKM08b]   Peter A. Boncz, Martin L. Kersten, and Stefan Manegold. Breaking the memory wall in MonetDB. Commun. ACM, 51(12):77–85, 2008.

[BLP11]   Spyros Blanas, Yinan Li, and Jignesh M. Patel. Design and evaluation of main memory hash join algorithms for multi-core cpus. In *Proceedings of the 2011 ACM SIGMOD International Conference on Management of data*, SIGMOD '11, pages 37–48, New York, NY, USA, 2011. ACM.

[BMK99]   Peter A. Boncz, Stefan Manegold, and Martin L. Kersten. Database architecture optimized for the new bottleneck: Memory access. In Malcolm P. Atkinson, Maria E. Orlowska, Patrick Valduriez, Stanley B. Zdonik, and Michael L. Brodie, editors, *VLDB'99, Proceedings of 25th International Conference on Very Large Data Bases, September 7-10, 1999, Edinburgh, Scotland, UK*, pages 54–65. Morgan Kaufmann, 1999.

[BN97]   Philip Bernstein and Eric Newcomer. Principles of transaction processing: for the systems professional. Morgan Kaufmann Publishers Inc., San Francisco, CA, USA, 1997.

[Bon02]   P. A. Boncz. Monet: A Next-Generation DBMS Kernel For Query-Intensive Applications. PhD thesis, Universiteit van Amsterdam, Amsterdam, The Netherlands, May 2002.

[BPASP11]   Kamil Bajda-Pawlikowski, Daniel J. Abadi, Avi Silberschatz, and Erik Paulson. Efficient processing of data warehousing queries in a split execution environment. In *Proceedings of the 2011 ACM SIGMOD International Conference on Management of Data*, SIGMOD '11, pages 1165–1176, New York, NY, USA, 2011. ACM.

[Bre00]   Eric A. Brewer. Towards robust distributed systems (abstract). In *Proceedings of the Nineteenth Annual ACM Symposium on Principles of Distributed Computing*, PODC '00, pages 7–, New York, NY, USA, 2000. ACM.

[Bre12]   Eric Brewer. Cap twelve years later: How the "rules" have changed. Computer, 45(2):23–29, 2012.

[BS13]   Zoltan Böszörmenyi and Hans-Jürgen Schönig. *PostgreSQL Replication*. Packt Publishing, 2013.

[BTAÖ13]   Cagri Balkesen, Jens Teubner, Gustavo Alonso, and M. Tamer Öszu. Main-memory hash joins on multi-core cpus: Tuning to the underlying hardware. In *Proceedings of the 29th Int'l Conference on Data Engineering (ICDE), Brisbane, Australia*, April 2013.

[Bur10]   Greg Burd. NoSQL. *login magazine*, 36(5), 2010.

[CAK+81]   D. D. Chamberlin, M. M. Astrahan, W. F. King, R. A. Lorie, J. W. Mehl, T. G. Price, M. Schkolnick, P. Griffiths Selinger, D. R. Slutz, B. W. Wade, and R. A. Yost. Support for repetitive transactions and ad hoc queries in system r. *ACM Trans. Database Syst.*, 6(1):70–94, March 1981.

[Cat11]   Rick Cattell. Scalable sql and nosql data stores. *SIGMOD Rec.*, 39(4):12–27, May 2011.

[CB74]   Donald D. Chamberlin and Raymond F. Boyce. Sequel: A structured english query language. In *Proceedings of the 1974 ACM SIGFIDET (now SIGMOD) workshop on Data description, access and control*, pages 249–264, New York, NY, USA, 1974. ACM.

[CC11]   Tom Coffind and Leona Coffing. *Tera-Tom on Teradata SQL V12/V13*. Coffing Publishing, 2011.

[CCS93]   E.F. Codd, S. B. Codd, and C. T. Salley. Providing olap (on-line analytical processing) to user-analysts: An it mandate. Technical report, E.F.Codd & Associates, 1993.

[CDG+06]   Fay Chang, Jeffrey Dean, Sanjay Ghemawat, Wilson C. Hsieh, Deborah A. Wallach, Mike Burrows, Tushar Chandra, Andrew Fikes, and Robert E. Gruber. Bigtable: A distributed storage system for structured data. In *Proceedings of the 7th USENIX Symposium on Operating Systems Design and Implementation - Volume 7*, OSDI '06, pages 15–15, Berkeley, CA, USA, 2006. USENIX Association.

[CG94]   Richard L. Cole and Goetz Graefe. Optimization of dynamic query evaluation plans. In *Proceedings of the 1994 ACM SIGMOD international conference on Management of data*, SIGMOD '94, pages 150–160, New York, NY, USA, 1994. ACM.

[CK85]   George P. Copeland and Setrag N. Khoshafian. A decomposition storage model. In *Proceedings of the 1985 ACM SIGMOD international conference on Management of data*, SIGMOD '85, pages 268–279, New York, NY, USA, 1985. ACM.

[CKP+93]   David Culler, Richard Karp, David Patterson, Abhijit Sahay, Klaus Erik Schauser, Eunice Santos, Ramesh Subramonian, and Thorsten von Eicken. Logp: Towards a realistic model of parallel computation. In *Proceedings of the Fourth ACM SIGPLAN Symposium on Principles and Practice of Parallel Programming*, PPOPP '93, pages 1–12, New York, NY, USA, 1993. ACM.

[CL86]   Michael J. Carey and Hongjun Lu. Load balancing in a locally distributed db system. In *Proceedings of the 1986 ACM SIGMOD international conference on Management of data*, SIGMOD '86, pages 108–119, New York, NY, USA, 1986. ACM.

[Cod70]   E. F. Codd. A relational model of data for large shared data banks. Commun. ACM, 13(6):377–387, 1970.

[Cor13]   Microsoft Corporation. Microsoft sql server-hadoop connector user guide. http://www.microsoft.com/en-us/download/details.aspx?id=27584, Last checked on July 23rd 2013.

[CST+10]   Brian F. Cooper, Adam Silberstein, Erwin Tam, Raghu Ramakrishnan, and Russell Sears. Benchmarking cloud serving systems with ycsb. In *SoCC '10: Proceedings of the 1st ACM symposium on Cloud computing*, pages 143–154, 2010.

[DF06]   Alex Davies and Harrison Fisk. *MySQL Clustering*. MySQL Press, 2006.

[DFI+13]   Cristian Diaconu, Craig Freedman, Erik Ismert, Per-Ake Larson, Pravin Mittal, Ryan Stonecipher, Nitin Verma, and Mike Zwilling. Hekaton: Sql server's memory-optimized oltp engine. In *Proceedings of the 2013 ACM SIGMOD International Conference on Management of Data*, SIGMOD '13, pages 1243–1254, New York, NY, USA, 2013. ACM.

[DG92]   David DeWitt and Jim Gray. Parallel database systems: the future of high perfor-
            mance database systems. *Commun. ACM*, 35(6):85–98, June 1992.

[DG08]   Jeffrey Dean and Sanjay Ghemawat. Mapreduce: Simplified data processing on
            large clusters. *Commun. ACM*, 51(1):107–113, January 2008.

[DGS+90]   D. J. Dewitt, S. Ghandeharizadeh, D. A. Schneider, A. Bricker, H. I. Hsiao, and
            R. Rasmussen. The gamma database machine project. IEEE Trans. on Knowl. and
            Data Eng., 2(1):44–62, March 1990.

[DHJ+07]   Giuseppe DeCandia, Deniz Hastorun, Madan Jampani, Gunavardhan Kakulapati,
            Avinash Lakshman, Alex Pilchin, Swaminathan Sivasubramanian, Peter Vosshall,
            and Werner Vogels. Dynamo: Amazon's highly available key-value store. In Pro-
            ceedings of Twenty-first ACM SIGOPS Symposium on Operating Systems Princi-
            ples, SOSP '07, pages 205–220, New York, NY, USA, 2007. ACM.

[DHN+13]   David J. DeWitt, Alan Halverson, Rimma Nehme, Srinath Shankar, Josep Aguilar-
            Saborit, Artin Avanes, Miro Flasza, and Jim Gramling. Split query processing in
            polybase. In Proceedings of the 2013 ACM SIGMOD International Conference on
            Management of Data, SIGMOD '13, pages 1255–1266, New York, NY, USA, 2013.
            ACM.

[DMS13]   D. J. DeWitt, S. Madden, and M. Stonebraker. How to Build a High-Performance
            Data Warehouse. http://db.lcs.mit.edu/madden/high_perf.pdf, Last checked on July
            23rd 2013.

[Doc13]   Microsoft SQL Server 2012 Documentation. xVelocity in SQL Server 2012. http://
            msdn.microsoft.com/en-us/library/hh922900.aspx, Last checked on July 23rd
            2013.

[EN10]   Ramez A. Elmasri and Shankrant B. Navathe. Fundamentals of Database Systems.
            Addison-Wesley Longman Publishing Co., Inc, Boston, MA, USA, 6th edition,
            2010.

[ERAEB05]   Hesham El-Rewini and Mostafa Abd-El-Barr. Advanced Computer Architecture and
            Parallel Processing (Wiley Series on Parallel and Distributed Computing). Wiley-
            Interscience, 2005.

[FCP+12]   Franz Färber, Sang Kyun Cha, Jürgen Primsch, Christof Bornhövd, Stefan Sigg,
            and Wolfgang Lehner. Sap hana database: data management for modern business
            applications. *SIGMOD Rec.*, 40(4):45–51, January 2012.

[FGKT10]   Philip Werner Frey, Romulo Goncalves, Martin L. Kersten, and Jens Teubner. A
            spinning join that does not get dizzy. In 2010 International Conference on Distributed
            Computing Systems, ICDCS 2010, Genova, Italy, June 21–25, 2010, pages 283–292,
            2010.

[Fit04]   Brad Fitzpatrick. Distributed caching with memcached. Linux J., 2004(124):5-,
            August 2004.

[FJK96]   Michael J. Franklin, Björn Thór Jónsson, and Donald Kossmann. Performance trade-
            offs for client-server query processing. In Proceedings of the 1996 ACM SIGMOD
            international conference on Management of data, SIGMOD '96, pages 149–160,
            New York, NY, USA, 1996. ACM.

[FML+12]   Franz Färber, Norman May, Wolfgang Lehner, Philipp Große, Ingo Müller, Hannes
            Rauhe, and Jonathan Dees. The SAP HANA Database - An Architecture Overview.
            IEEE Data Eng. Bull., 35(1):28–33, 2012.

[GCMK+12]   Martin Grund, Philippe Cudré-Mauroux, Jens Krüger, Samuel Madden, and Hasso
            Plattner. An overview of hyrise - a main memory hybrid storage engine. IEEE Data
            Eng. Bull., 35(1):52–57, 2012.

[GGL03]   Sanjay Ghemawat, Howard Gobioff, and Shun-Tak Leung. The google file system. In
            Proceedings of the Nineteenth ACM Symposium on Operating Systems Principles,
            SOSP '03, pages 29–43, New York, NY, USA, 2003. ACM.

[GGS96]   Sumit Ganguly, Akshay Goel, and Avi Silberschatz. Efficient and accurate cost
            models for parallel query optimization (extended abstract). In Proceedings of the
            fifteenth ACM SIGACT-SIGMOD-SIGART symposium on Principles of database
            systems, PODS '96, pages 172–181, New York, NY, USA, 1996. ACM.

[GIG13]   GIGABYTE - Motherboard, Graphics Card, Notebook, Server and More. http://www.gigabyte.us, Last checked on July 23rd 2013.

[GK85]   Dieter Gawlick and David Kinkade. Varieties of concurrency control in ims/vs fast path. IEEE Database Eng. Bull., 8(2):3–10, 1985.

[GK10]   Romulo Goncalves and Martin L. Kersten. The data cyclotron query processing scheme. In EDBT 2010, 13th International Conference on Extending Database Technology, Lausanne, Switzerland, March 22–26, 2010, Proceedings, pages 75–86, 2010.

[GK11]   Romulo Goncalves and Martin Kersten. The data cyclotron query processing scheme. ACM Trans. Database Syst., 36(4):27:1–27:35, December 2011.

[GKP+10]   Martin Grund, Jens Krüger, Hasso Plattner, Philippe Cudre-Mauroux, and Samuel Madden. Hyrise: a main memory hybrid storage engine. Proc. VLDB Endow., 4(2):105–116, November 2010.

[GMS92]   H. Garcia-Molina and K. Salem. Main memory database systems: An overview. IEEE Trans. on Knowl. and Data Eng., 4(6):509–516, December 1992.

[GMUW08]   Hector Garcia-Molina, Jeffrey D. Ullman, and Jennifer Widom. Database Systems: The Complete Book. Prentice Hall Press, Upper Saddle River, NJ, USA, 2 edition, 2008.

[Gra94a]   G. Graefe. Volcano&#151 an extensible and parallel query evaluation system. IEEE Trans. on Knowl. and Data Eng., 6(1):120–135, February 1994.

[Gra94b]   Goetz Graefe. Volcano - an extensible and parallel query evaluation system. IEEE Trans. Knowl. Data Eng., 6(1):120–135, 1994.

[GS02]   Meeta Gupta and C. Anita Sastry. Storage Area Network Fundamentals. Cisco Press, 2002.

[HF86]   Robert Brian Hagmann and Domenico Ferrari. Performance analysis of several back-end database architectures. ACM Trans. Database Syst., 11(1):1–26, March 1986.

[Hil90]   Mark D. Hill. What is scalability? SIGARCH Comput. Archit. News, 18(4):18–21, December 1990.

[HLM+11]   Theo Härder, Wolfgang Lehner, Bernhard Mitschang, Harald Schöning, and Holger Schwarz, editors. Datenbanksysteme für Business, Technologie und Web (BTW), 14. Fachtagung des GI-Fachbereichs "Datenbanken und Informationssysteme" (DBIS), 2.-4.3.2011 in Kaiserslautern, Germany, volume 180 of LNI. GI, 2011.

[HM95]   Waqar Hasan and Rajeev Motwani. Coloring away communication in parallel query optimization. In Proceedings of the 21th International Conference on Very Large Data Bases, VLDB '95, pages 239–250, San Francisco, CA, USA, 1995. Morgan Kaufmann Publishers Inc.

[Hog13]   Mike Hogan. Shared-Disk vs. Shared-Nothing - Comparing Architectures for Clustered Databases. http://www.scaledb.com/pdfs/WP_SDvSN.pdf, Last checked on July 23rd 2013.

[HP11]   John L. Hennessy and David A. Patterson. Computer Architecture, Fifth Edition: A Quantitative Approach. Morgan Kaufmann Publishers Inc., San Francisco, CA, USA, 5th edition, 2011.

[HS13]   Donald J. Haderle and Cynthia M. Saracco. The history and growth of ibm's db2. IEEE Annals of the History of Computing, 35(2):54–66, 2013.

[HSW+04]   Larry Huston, Rahul Sukthankar, Rajiv Wickremesinghe, M. Satyanarayanan, Gregory R. Ganger, Erik Riedel, and Anastassia Ailamaki. Diamond: A storage architecture for early discard in interactive search. In Proceedings of the 3rd USENIX Conference on File and Storage Technologies, FAST '04, pages 73–86, Berkeley, CA, USA, 2004. USENIX Association.

[IBM13]   IBM. DB2 pureScale. http://www.ibm.com/software/data/db2/linux-unix-windows/purescale/, Last checked on July 23rd 2013.

[ILFL12]   Sadeka Islam, Kevin Lee, Alan Fekete, and Anna Liu. How a consumer can measure elasticity for cloud platforms. In Proceedings of the 3rd ACM/SPEC International

Conference on Performance Engineering, ICPE '12, pages 85–96, New York, NY, USA, 2012. ACM.

[Int13]   Intel Coporation. Intel automated relational knowledgebase. http://ark.intel.com, Last checked on July 1st 2013.

[Jac13]   Dean Jacobs. Dean's Blog: After reviewing some cloud database papers. http://deanbjacobs.wordpress.com/2010/08/12/cloudpaperreviews/, Last checked on July 23rd 2013.

[KC04]   Ralph Kimball and Joe Caserta. The Data Warehouse ETL Toolkit: Practical Techniques for Extracting, Cleaning, Conforming, and Delivering Data. Wiley, Indianapolis, IN, 2004.

[KD98]   Navin Kabra and David J. DeWitt. Efficient mid-query re-optimization of suboptimal query execution plans. In Proceedings of the 1998 ACM SIGMOD international conference on Management of data, SIGMOD '98, pages 106–117, New York, NY, USA, 1998. ACM.

[Kee99]   Kimberly Kristine Keeton. Computer Architecture Support For Database Applications. PhD thesis, University of California at Berkeley, 1999.

[KGT06]   Andreas Knoepfel, Bernhard Groene, and Peter Tabeling. Fundamental Modeling Concepts: Effective Communication of IT Systems. John Wiley & Sons, 2006.

[KGT+10]   Jens Krueger, Martin Grund, Christian Tinnefeld, Hasso Plattner, and Franz Faerber. Optimizing write performance for read optimized databases. In Proceedings of the 15th international conference on Database Systems for Advanced Applications - Volume Part II, DASFAA'10, pages 291–305, Berlin, Heidelberg, 2010. Springer-Verlag.

[Kir96]   John Kirkwood. SYBASE SQL Server II. International Thomson Publishing Company, 1st edition, 1996.

[KKG+11]   Jens Krueger, Changkyu Kim, Martin Grund, Nadathur Satish, David Schwalb, Jatin Chhugani, Hasso Plattner, and Pradeep Dubey. Fast updates on read-optimized databases using multi-core cpus. Proc. VLDB Endow., 5(1):61–72, September 2011.

[KKN+08]   Robert Kallman, Hideaki Kimura, Jonathan Natkins, Andrew Pavlo, Alexander Rasin, Stanley Zdonik, Evan P. C. Jones, Samuel Madden, Michael Stonebraker, Yang Zhang, John Hugg, and Daniel J. Abadi. H-Store: a high-performance, distributed main memory transaction processing system. Proc. VLDB Endow., 1(2):1496–1499, 2008.

[KLB+12]   Barbara Klein, Richard Alan Long, Kenneth Ray Blackman, Diane Lynne Goff, Stephen Paul Nathan, Moira McFadden Lanyi, Margaret M. Wilson, John Butterweck, and Sandra L. Sherrill. An Introduction to IMS: Your Complete Guide to IBM Information Management System. IBM Press, 2nd edition, 2012.

[Klo10]   Rusty Klophaus. Riak core: Building distributed applications without shared state. In ACM SIGPLAN Commercial Users of Functional Programming, CUFP '10, pages 14:1–14:1, New York, NY, USA, 2010. ACM.

[KNI+11]   Alfons Kemper, Thomas Neumann, Fakultät Für Informatik, Technische Universität München, and D-Garching. Hyper: A hybrid oltp & olap main memory database system based on virtual memory snapshots. In In ICDE, 2011.

[Kos00]   Donald Kossmann. The state of the art in distributed query processing. ACM Comput. Surv., 32(4):422–469, December 2000.

[KPH98]   Kimberly Keeton, David A. Patterson, and Joseph M. Hellerstein. A case for intelligent disks (idisks). SIGMOD Rec., 27(3):42–52, September 1998.

[KTGP10]   Jens Krueger, Christian Tinnefeld, Martin Grund, and Hasso Plattner. A case for online mixed workload processing. In Proceedings of the Third International Workshop on Testing Database Systems, DBTest '10, pages 8:1–8:6, New York, NY, USA, 2010. ACM.

[Lam78]   Leslie Lamport. Time, clocks, and the ordering of events in a distributed system. Commun. ACM, 21(7):558–565, July 1978.

[LCF+13]   Per-Ake Larson, Cipri Clinciu, Campbell Fraser, Eric N. Hanson, Mostafa Mokhtar, Michal Nowakiewicz, Vassilis Papadimos, Susan L. Price, Srikumar Rangarajan, Remus Rusanu, and Mayukh Saubhasik. Enhancements to sql server column stores. In Proceedings of the 2013 ACM SIGMOD International Conference on Management of Data, SIGMOD '13, pages 1159–1168, New York, NY, USA, 2013. ACM.

[LFV+12]   Andrew Lamb, Matt Fuller, Ramakrishna Varadarajan, Nga Tran, Ben Vandiver, Lyric Doshi, and Chuck Bear. The vertica analytic database: C-store 7 years later. *Proc. VLDB Endow.*, 5(12):1790–1801, August 2012.

[LKF+13]   Juchang Lee, Yong Sik Kwon, Franz Farber, Michael Muehle, Chulwon Lee, Christian Bensberg, Joo Yeon Lee, Arthur H. Lee, and Wolfgang Lehner. Sap hana distributed in-memory database system: Transaction, session, and metadata management. 2013 IEEE 29th International Conference on Data Engineering (ICDE), 0:1165–1173, 2013.

[LLS13]   Justin J. Levandoski, David B. Lomet, and Sudipta Sengupta. The bw-tree: A b-tree for new hardware platforms. 2013 IEEE 29th International Conference on Data Engineering (ICDE), pages 302–313, 2013.

[LM10]   Avinash Lakshman and Prashant Malik. Cassandra: A decentralized structured storage system. *SIGOPS Oper. Syst. Rev.*, 44(2):35–40, April 2010.

[LS90]   Eliezer Levy and Abraham Silberschatz. Distributed file systems: Concepts and examples. *ACM Comput. Surv.*, 22(4):321–374, December 1990.

[LVZ93]   Rosana S. G. Lanzelotte, Patrick Valduriez, and Mohamed Zaït. On the effectiveness of optimization search strategies for parallel execution spaces. In Proceedings of the 19th International Conference on Very Large Data Bases, VLDB '93, pages 493–504, San Francisco, CA, USA, 1993. Morgan Kaufmann Publishers Inc.

[Mat01]   S. Matsuda. Theoretical limitations of a hopfield network for crossbar switching. *Trans. Neur. Netw.*, 12(3):456–462, May 2001.

[MBK02a]   Stefan Manegold, Peter Boncz, and Martin L. Kersten. Generic database cost models for hierarchical memory systems. In Proceedings of the 28th international conference on Very Large Data Bases, VLDB '02, pages 191–202. VLDB Endowment, 2002.

[MBK02b]   Stefan Manegold, Peter Boncz, and Martin L. Kersten. Generic database cost models for hierarchical memory systems. In Proceedings of the 28th international conference on Very Large Data Bases, VLDB '02, pages 191–202. VLDB Endowment, 2002.

[MBK02c]   Stefan Manegold, Peter Boncz, and Martin L. Kersten. Generic database cost models for hierarchical memory systems. Technical Report INS-R0203, CWI, Amsterdam, The Netherlands, March 2002.

[MC13]   Masood Mortazavi Yanchen Liu Stephen Morgan Aniket Adnaik Mengmeng Chen, Fang Cao. Distributed query processing with monetdb. In 7th Extremely Large Databases Conference (XLDB), 2013.

[ME13]   The Register Martin Edwards. Texas Memory RamSan-440 Texas Memory Systems Makes Mighty Big RAM SSD. http://www.theregister.co.uk/2008/07/22/texas_memory_systems_ramsan_440/, Last checked on July 23rd 2013.

[Mel13]   Mellanox Technologies. RDMA Aware Networks Programming User Manual, V1.4 2013.

[mem13a]   memcached - a distributed memory object caching system. http://memcached.org, Last checked on July 23rd 2013.

[Mem13b]   Stratosphere Project Members. Stratosphere. http://www.stratosphere.eu, Last checked on July 23rd 2013.

[MGL+10]   Sergey Melnik, Andrey Gubarev, Jing Jing Long, Geoffrey Romer, Shiva Shivakumar, Matt Tolton, and Theo Vassilakis. Dremel: interactive analysis of web-scale datasets. *Proc. VLDB Endow.*, 3(1-2):330–339, September 2010.

[Mic02]   Maged M. Michael. High performance dynamic lock-free hash tables and list-based sets. In Proceedings of the fourteenth annual ACM symposium on Parallel algorithms and architectures, SPAA '02, pages 73–82, New York, NY, USA, 2002. ACM.

[MN92]   C. Mohan and Inderpal Narang. Efficient locking and caching of data in the multi-system shard disks transaction environment. In Alain Pirotte, Claude Delobel, and Georg Gottlob, editors, Advances in Database Technology - EDBT'92, 3rd International Conference on Extending Database Technology, Vienna, Austria, March 23–27, 1992, Proceedings, volume 580 of Lecture Notes in Computer Science, pages 453–468. Springer, 1992.

[Moo65]   G. E. Moore. Cramming More Components onto Integrated Circuits. *Electronics*, 38(8):114–117, April 1965.

[Moo11]   Trevor Moore. The Sybase IQ Survival Guide, Versions 12.6 through to 15.2. [Lulu], 1. ed. edition, 2011. by Trevor Moore.

[MRR+13]   Tobias Mühlbauer, Wolf Rödiger, Angelika Reiser, Alfons Kemper, and Thomas Neumann. Scyper: elastic olap throughput on transactional data. In Proceedings of the Second Workshop on Data Analytics in the Cloud, DanaC '13, pages 11–15, New York, NY, USA, 2013. ACM.

[MSFD11a]   Héctor Montaner, Federico Silla, Holger Fröning, and José Duato. Memscale: in-cluster-memory databases. In Proceedings of the 20th ACM international conference on Information and knowledge management, CIKM '11, pages 2569–2572, New York, NY, USA, 2011. ACM.

[MSFD11b]   Héctor Montaner, Federico Silla, Holger Fröning, and José Duato. Memscale^{tm}: A scalable environment for databases. In Parimala Thulasiraman, Laurence Tianruo Yang, Qiwen Pan, Xingang Liu, Yaw-Chung Chen, Yo-Ping Huang, Lin-Huang Chang, Che-Lun Hung, Che-Rung Lee, Justin Y. Shi, and Ying Zhang, editors, HPCC, pages 339–346. IEEE, 2011.

[MWV+13]   Marko Milek, Antoni Wolski, Katriina Vakkila, Dan Behman, Samir Gupta, and John Seery. Ibm soliddb: Delivering data with extreme speed. http://www-01.ibm.com/support/docview.wss?uid=swg27020436&aid=1, Last checked on July 23rd 2013.

[MyS13a]   MySQL Team. Mysql internals manual - writing a custom storage engine. http://dev.mysql.com/doc/internals/en/custom-engine.html, Last checked on July 23rd 2013.

[MyS13b]   MySQL Team. MySQL - The world's most popular open source database. http://www.mysql.com/, Last checked on Sep 17th 2013.

[Neu11]   Thomas Neumann. Efficiently compiling efficient query plans for modern hardware. *Proc. VLDB Endow.*, 4(9):539–550, June 2011.

[new13]   Newegg.com - computer parts, laptops, electornics. http://newegg.com, Prices checked on Sep 21st 2013.

[NFG+13]   Rajesh Nishtala, Hans Fugal, Steven Grimm, Marc Kwiatkowski, Herman Lee, Harry C. Li, Ryan McElroy, Mike Paleczny, Daniel Peek, Paul Saab, David Stafford, Tony Tung, and Venkateshwaran Venkataramani. Scaling memcache at facebook. In Proceedings of the 10th USENIX Conference on Networked Systems Design and Implementation, nsdi'13, pages 385–398, Berkeley, CA, USA, 2013. USENIX Association.

[NL06]   Linda Null and Julia Lobur. The Essentials of Computer Organization And Architecture. Jones and Bartlett Publishers Inc, USA, 2006.

[OAE+11]   John K. Ousterhout, Parag Agrawal, David Erickson, Christos Kozyrakis, Jacob Leverich, David Mazières, Subhasish Mitra, Aravind Narayanan, Diego Ongaro, Guru M. Parulkar, Mendel Rosenblum, Stephen M. Rumble, Eric Stratmann, and Ryan Stutsman. The case for RAMCloud. Commun. ACM, 54(7):121–130, 2011.

[OCD+88]   John K. Ousterhout, Andrew R. Cherenson, Fred Douglis, Michael N. Nelson, and Brent B. Welch. The sprite network operating system. IEEE Computer, 21(2):23–36, 1988.

[O'N]   O'Neil, P. E. and O'Neil, E. J. and Chen, X. The Star Schema Benchmark (SSB).

[ORS+11]   Diego Ongaro, Stephen M. Rumble, Ryan Stutsman, John K. Ousterhout, and
             Mendel Rosenblum. Fast crash recovery in RAMCloud. In Proceedings of the 23rd
             ACM Symposium on Operating Systems Principles 2011, SOSP 2011, Cascais,
             Portugal, October 23–26, 2011, pages 29–41. ACM, 2011.

[ÖV11]   M. Tamer Özsu and Patrick Valduriez. Principles of Distributed Database Systems,
             Third Edition. Springer, 2011.

[PH08]   David A. Patterson and John L. Hennessy. Computer Organization and Design,
             Fourth Edition, Fourth Edition: The Hardware/Software Interface (The Morgan
             Kaufmann Series in Computer Architecture and Design). Morgan Kaufmann Pub-
             lishers Inc., San Francisco, CA, USA, 4th edition, 2008.

[Pil12]   Markus Pilman. Running a transactional database on top of ramcloud. Master's
             thesis, ETH Zürich, Department of Computer Science, 2012.

[Pla09]   Hasso Plattner. A common database approach for oltp and olap using an in-memory
             column database. In Proceedings of the 2009 ACM SIGMOD International Con-
             ference on Management of data, SIGMOD '09, pages 1–2, New York, NY, USA,
             2009. ACM.

[Pla11a]   Hasso Plattner. In-Memory Data Management - An Inflection Point for Enterprise
             Applications. Springer-Verlag, Berlin Heidelberg, 2011.

[Pla11b]   Hasso Plattner. Sanssoucidb: An in-memory database for processing enterprise
             workloads. In Härder et al. [HLM+11], pages 2–21.

[Pos13]   Postgres-XC Team. Postgres-XC (eXtensible Cluster) Wiki. http://postgres-xc.
             sourceforge.net, Last checked on October 2nd 2013.

[Raa93]   Francois Raab. Tpc-c - the standard benchmark for online transaction processing
             (oltp). In Jim Gray, editor, The Benchmark Handbook. Morgan Kaufmann, 1993.

[Rah93]   Erhard Rahm. Parallel query processing in shared disk database systems. SIGMOD
             Rec., 22(4):32–37, December 1993.

[RGF98]   Erik Riedel, Garth A. Gibson, and Christos Faloutsos. Active storage for large-scale
             data mining and multimedia. In Proceedings of the 24rd International Conference on
             Very Large Data Bases, VLDB '98, pages 62–73, San Francisco, CA, USA, 1998.
             Morgan Kaufmann Publishers Inc.

[ROS+11]   Stephen M. Rumble, Diego Ongaro, Ryan Stutsman, Mendel Rosenblum, and John
             K. Ousterhout. It's time for low latency. In Proceedings of the 13th USENIX con-
             ference on Hot topics in operating systems, HotOS'13, pages 11–11, Berkeley, CA,
             USA, 2011. USENIX Association.

[RS13]   David Daoud for IDC Rajani Singh. Intel announces 4q12 earnings: Perfor-
             mance assessment and the road ahead. http://www.idc.com/getdoc.jsp?containerId=
             lcUS23915413, Last checked on July 23rd 2013.

[RSI07]   Aravindan Raghuveer, Steven W. Schlosser, and Sami Iren. Enabling database-aware
             storage with osd. Mass Storage Systems and Technologies, IEEE / NASA Goddard
             Conference on, 0:129–142, 2007.

[SAB+05]   Mike Stonebraker, Daniel J. Abadi, Adam Batkin, Xuedong Chen, Mitch Cherniack,
             Miguel Ferreira, Edmond Lau, Amerson Lin, Sam Madden, Elizabeth O'Neil, Pat
             O'Neil, Alex Rasin, Nga Tran, and Stan Zdonik. C-store: a column-oriented dbms.
             In Proceedings of the 31st international conference on Very large data bases, VLDB
             '05, pages 553–564. VLDB Endowment, 2005.

[SAP13]   SAP AG. SAP HANA Administration Guides. http://help.sap.com/hana_platform,
             Last checked on July 23rd 2013.

[SBADAD05]   Muthian Sivathanu, Lakshmi N. Bairavasundaram, Andrea C. Arpaci-Dusseau, and
             Remzi H. Arpaci-Dusseau. Database-aware semantically-smart storage. In Proceed-
             ings of the 4th conference on USENIX Conference on File and Storage Technologies
             - Volume 4, FAST'05, pages 18–18, Berkeley, CA, USA, 2005. USENIX Associa-
             tion.

[Sca13]   ScaleDB Team. ScaleDB for MySQL - Technical Overview. http://scaledb.com/
            pdfs/TechnicalOverview.pdf, Last checked on July 23rd 2013.

[Sch13]   Jan Schaffner. Multi Tenancy for Cloud-Based In-Memory Column Databases. PhD
            thesis, Hasso-Plattner-Institut, 2013.

[SD89]   Donovan A. Schneider and David J. DeWitt. A performance evaluation of four
            parallel join algorithms in a shared-nothing multiprocessor environment. In Pro-
            ceedings of the 1989 ACM SIGMOD international conference on Management of
            data, SIGMOD '89, pages 110–121, New York, NY, USA, 1989. ACM.

[Ser13]   Amazon Web Services. SAP HANA One on Amazon Web Services. https://aws.
            amazon.com/marketplace/pp/B009KA3CRY, Last checked on July 23rd 2013.

[SG13]   ETH Zürich Systems Group. Department of computer science at eth zurich: Systems
            group. http://www.systems.ethz.ch/, Last checked on July 23rd 2013.

[SGK+88]   R. Sandberg, D. Golgberg, S. Kleiman, D. Walsh, and B. Lyon. Innovations in inter-
            networking. chapter Design and Implementation of the Sun Network Filesystem,
            pages 379–390. Artech House Inc, Norwood, MA, USA, 1988.

[SGM90]   K. Salem and H. Garcia-Molina. System m: A transaction processing testbed for
            memory resident data. IEEE Trans. on Knowl. and Data Eng., 2(1):161–172, March
            1990.

[SH02]   Frank Schmuck and Roger Haskin. Gpfs: A shared-disk file system for large com-
            puting clusters. In Proceedings of the 1st USENIX Conference on File and Storage
            Technologies, FAST '02, Berkeley, CA, USA, 2002. USENIX Association.

[SJK+13]   Jan Schaffner, Tim Januschowski, Megan Kercher, Tim Kraska, Hasso Plattner,
            Michael J. Franklin, and Dean Jacobs. Rtp: robust tenant placement for elastic
            in-memory database clusters. In Proceedings of the ACM SIGMOD International
            Conference on Management of Data, SIGMOD 2013, New York, NY, USA, June
            22–27, 2013, pages 773–784, 2013.

[SKG+12]   Roshan Sumbaly, Jay Kreps, Lei Gao, Alex Feinberg, Chinmay Soman, and Sam
            Shah. Serving large-scale batch computed data with project voldemort. In Proceed-
            ings of the 10th USENIX Conference on File and Storage Technologies, FAST'12,
            pages 18–18, Berkeley, CA, USA, 2012. USENIX Association.

[SKRC10]   Konstantin Shvachko, Hairong Kuang, Sanjay Radia, and Robert Chansler. The
            hadoop distributed file system. In Proceedings of the 2010 IEEE 26th Symposium
            on Mass Storage Systems and Technologies (MSST), MSST '10, pages 1–10, Wash-
            ington, DC, USA, 2010. IEEE Computer Society.

[SMHW02]   Daniel J. Sorin, Milo M. K. Martin, Mark D. Hill, and David A. Wood. Safe-
            tynet: improving the availability of shared memory multiprocessors with global
            checkpoint/recovery. In Proceedings of the 29th annual international symposium on
            Computer architecture, ISCA '02, pages 123–134, Washington, DC, USA, 2002.
            IEEE Computer Society.

[Smi13]   Zack Smith. Bandwidth: a memory bandwidth benchmark. http://home.comcast.
            net/veritas/bandwidth.html, Last checked on July 1st 2013.

[SOE+12]   Jeff Shute, Mircea Oancea, Stephan Ellner, Ben Handy, Eric Rollins, Bart Samwel,
            Radek Vingralek, Chad Whipkey, Xin Chen, Beat Jegerlehner, Kyle Littlefield,
            and Phoenix Tong. F1: the fault-tolerant distributed rdbms supporting google's ad
            business. In Proceedings of the ACM SIGMOD International Conference on Man-
            agement of Data, SIGMOD 2012, Scottsdale, AZ, USA, May 20–24, 2012, pages
            777–778, 2012.

[sta04]   American National Standards Institute (ANSI) T10 standard. Information technol-
            ogy - scsi object-based storage device commands (osd). Standard ANSI/INCITS
            400-2004, December 2004.

[Sto87]   Michael Stonebraker. The design of the postgres storage system. In Proceedings
            of the 13th International Conference on Very Large Data Bases, VLDB '87, pages
            289–300, San Francisco, CA, USA, 1987. Morgan Kaufmann Publishers Inc.

[Sut05]   Herb Sutter. The Free Lunch Is Over: A Fundamental Turn Toward Concurrency in Software. Dr. Dobb's Journal, 30(3), 2005.

[SW13]   Michael Stonebraker and Ariel Weisberg. The voltdb main memory dbms. IEEE Data Eng. Bull., 36(2):21–27, 2013.

[Syb13a]   Sybase - An SAP Company. SAP Sybase IQ. http://www.sybase.com/products/datawarehousing/sybaseiq, Last checked on July 23rd 2013.

[Syb13b]   Sybase - An SAP Company. A Practical Hardware Sizing Guide for Sybase IQ 15. http://www.sybase.de/files/White_Papers/Sybase_IQ_15_SizingGuide_wp.pdf, Last checked on Nov 1st 2013.

[Tan07]   Andrew S. Tanenbaum. Modern Operating Systems. Prentice Hall Press, Upper Saddle River, NJ, USA, 3rd edition, 2007.

[Ter13]   Teradata. Teradata Active Enterprise Data Warehouse 6650. http://www.teradata.com/brochures/Teradata-Active-Enterprise-Data-Warehouse-6650/, Last checked on July 23rd 2013.

[The13]   The Embedded Microprocessor Benchmark Consortium. The coremark benchmark. http://www.eembc.org/coremark, Last checked on September 1st 2013.

[Tho02]   Erik Thomsen. Olap Solutions: Building Multidimensional Information Systems. John Wiley & Sons Inc, New York, NY, USA, 2nd edition, 2002.

[Tho11]   Michael E. Thomadakis. The architecture of the nehalem processor and the architecture of the nehalem processor and nehalem-ep smp platforms. Research Report at the University of Texas, 2011.

[Tin09]   Christian Tinnefeld. Application characteristics of enterprise applications. Master's thesis, Hasso-Plattner-Institut, Potsdam, Germany, 2009.

[TKBP14]   Christian Tinnefeld, Donald Kossmann, Joos-Hendrik Boese, and Hasso Plattner. Parallel join executions in ramcloud. In CloudDB - In conjunction with ICDE 2014, 2014.

[TKG+13]   Christian Tinnefeld, Donald Kossmann, Martin Grund, Joos-Hendrik Boese, Frank Renkes, Vishal Sikka, and Hasso Plattner. Elastic online analytical processing on ramcloud. In Proceedings of the 16th International Conference on Extending Database Technology, EDBT '13, pages 454–464, New York, NY, USA, 2013. ACM.

[TMK+11]   Christian Tinnefeld, Stephan Müller, Helen Kaltegärtner, Sebastian Hillig, Lars Butzmann, David Eickhoff, Stefan Klauck, Daniel Taschik, Björn Wagner, Oliver Xylander, Hasso Plattner, and Cafer Tosun. Available-to-promise on an in-memory column store. In Härder et al. [HLM+11], pages 667–686.

[TMKG09]   Christian Tinnefeld, Stephan Müller, Jens Krüger, and Martin Grund. Leveraging multi-core cpus in the context of demand planning. In 16th International Conference on Industrial Engineering and Engineering Management (IEEM), Beijing, China, 2009.

[TP11a]   Christian Tinnefeld and Hasso Plattner. Cache-conscious data placement in an in-memory key-value store. In IDEAS 2011: 15th International Database Engineering and Applications Symposium, 2011.

[TP11b]   Christian Tinnefeld and Hasso Plattner. Exploiting memory locality in distributed key-value stores. In ICDE Workshops 2011, 2011.

[TS90]   Shreekant S. Thakkar and Mark Sweiger. Performance of an oltp application on symmetry multiprocessor system. In Proceedings of the 17th annual international symposium on Computer Architecture, ISCA '90, pages 228–238, New York, NY, USA, 1990. ACM.

[TSJ+09]   Ashish Thusoo, Joydeep Sen Sarma, Namit Jain, Zheng Shao, Prasad Chakka, Suresh Anthony, Hao Liu, Pete Wyckoff, and Raghotham Murthy. Hive: A warehousing solution over a map-reduce framework. Proc. VLDB Endow., 2(2):1626–1629, August 2009.

[TTP13]   Christian Tinnefeld, Daniel Taschik, and Hasso Plattner. Providing high-availability and elasticity for an in-memory database system with ramcloud. In GI-Jahrestagung, pages 472–486, 2013.

[TTP14]   Christian Tinnefeld, Daniel Taschik, and Hasso Plattner. Quantifying the elasticity
            of a database management system. In DBKDA, 2014.
[Tur90]   Efraim Turban. Decision Support and Expert Systems: Management Support Sys-
            tems. Prentice Hall PTR, Upper Saddle River, NJ, USA, 2nd edition, 1990.
[TWP12]   Christian Tinnefeld, Björn Wagner, and Hasso Plattner. Operating on hierarchical
            enterprise data in an in-memory column store. In DBKDA, 2012.
[UFA98]   Tolga Urhan, Michael J. Franklin, and Laurent Amsaleg. Cost-based query scram-
            bling for initial delays. In Proceedings of the 1998 ACM SIGMOD international
            conference on Management of data, SIGMOD '98, pages 130–141, New York, NY,
            USA, 1998. ACM.
[Ver13]   HP Vertica. Native BI, ETL, & Hadoop/MapReduce Integration. http://www.vertica.
            com/the-analytics-platform/native-bi-etl-and-hadoop-mapreduce-integration/,
            Last checked on July 23rd 2013.
[vN93]   John von Neumann. First draft of a report on the edvac. IEEE Ann. Hist. Comput.,
            15(4):27–75, October 1993.
[Vog07]   Werner Vogels. Data access patterns in the amazon.com technology platform. In
            Proceedings of the 33rd International Conference on Very Large Data Bases, VLDB
            '07, pages 1–1. VLDB Endowment, 2007.
[Wei84]   Reinhold P. Weicker. Dhrystone: a synthetic systems programming benchmark.
            Commun. ACM, 27(10):1013–1030, October 1984.
[Whi09]   Tom White. Hadoop: The Definitive Guide. O'Reilly Media Inc, 1st edition, 2009.
[WH 1]   Antoni Wolski and Sally Hartnell. soliddb and the secrets of speed. IBM Data
            Magazine, 2010 Issue 1.
[WW13]   Microsoft Windows HPC Team Wenhao Wu. Overview of rdma on win-
            dows. https://www.openfabrics.org/ofa-documents/doc_download/222-microsoft-
            overview-of-rdma-on-windows.html, Last checked on July 23rd 2013.
[Zem12]   Fred Zemke. Whats new in sql:2011. SIGMOD Rec., 41(1):67–73, April 2012.

Printed in the United States
By Bookmasters